RAW FOOD ART

Four Seasons of Plant-Powered Goodness

First Edition Published in the United States of America 2016

www.OlenkosKitchen.com

Library of Congress Cataloging-in-Publication Data available upon request.

ISBN 9780997105919

Raw Food Art may be purchased for educational, business, or promotional use.
For information on bulk purchases, please contact the sales department at sales@olenkoskitchen.com.

Some of the recipes and photographs have appeared in print or digital form.

All photography by Bill Winters and Aleksandra Winters

Book design by Crave Creative Group

Editing by Nicole Wayland of Ford Editing

First Edition: March 2016

Food is energy.
Food is life.
Food is medicine.

Cooking is so much fun, and the kitchen is one of the best places to be.

I was inspired by Mother Nature and the four seasons to create these recipes.

This book is dedicated to my Polish grandmother, Zofia. Since I was a small child, she inspired me to respect and love nature. She taught me to use food as medicine. I also dedicate this book to my mom, Anna, who is my greatest teacher in the kitchen.

Special thanks to my talented, creative, and loving husband, Bill, for always believing in my vision and for his amazing photography.

Love, kisses, and hugs to my magical little chefs - my two cats, Sushi and Kizia Mizia - for surrounding our kitchen with joy and unconditional love.

Many thanks and gratitude to all those wonderful, loving, and inspirational people in my life - my family, friends, students, and all of my teachers.

Much appreciation to my team - Heather, Nicole, Lidia, Jay, and Robert - for your incredible work and attention to detail.

Live, Love, Light, and Fruits from

Olenko's Kitchen

Contents

Summer

Autumn

Hello, Beautiful!

With every journey, there's always a beginning. I started cooking when I was five years old. I used to watch my mother and grandmother harvest fruits and vegetables from our garden in Poland and make healthy and delicious meals. We ate real food—it wasn't called organic back then, but it was wholesome and full of flavor. I remember playing in the garden, pretending I had a food store or café and "making" my own "food" from flowers, leaves, fruits, and vegetables. Years later, I am reliving my childhood make-believe as an adult, and I'm so happy to have the opportunity to share my passion with you.

If you like simple, real, delicious, homegrown food that's colorful, flavorful, and creative, you'll love the recipes in this book! I truly believe that everyone can cook. I don't like to follow any rules, and my philosophy is simple: I want to enjoy my life, and I want to enjoy my food. When I travel, I take cooking classes, go to local farms, and talk to locals about how they prepare their food. I'm very inspired by different cultures. My food is very eclectic and a bit unconventional, but it's healthy and good for the mind, body, and spirit.

This book will show you how to make delicious and nutritious food inspired by art and nature. Get inspired by nature and be grateful for the abundance of amazing plants, fruits, greens, and veggies that Mother Nature has to offer. Our bodies have the ability to heal and to thrive when we fuel it properly—meaning food, water, rest, and inner peace. When we are in harmony with nature, our lives work better. Being connected to the earth and to our food is tremendously important for our health and happiness. So, embrace your inner chef. Go back to the basics and find true beauty in real, simple food. Find joy in cooking your own food. Be in harmony with nature, with the seasons, and with life. Your individual style will come with time—just get busy in the kitchen!

Let's get started!

What is Raw Food?

Raw food is food that has not been heated above 118°F. Food cooked over this temperature loses much of its nutritional value, whereas raw, living food retains its natural enzymes, which are critical to our health. Enzymes are the power of life. The philosophy of eating a raw diet is simple: the more raw food you eat, the better your overall health, because your food has retained more of its essential nutrients. Uncooked, organic, unprocessed foods are vital for a healthy immune system—to help fight chronic diseases and allow our bodies to thrive. Strive to eat plenty of fresh, raw fruits, vegetables, greens, nuts, seeds, and sprouted beans and grains. Embracing a raw, plant-based diet is easy and fun—there's really so much you can do.

I believe that using quality ingredients is essential to creating great-tasting food, and that they are even more important when preparing raw food. When preparing the recipes in this book, use seasonal, ripe, organic, and fresh ingredients for your meals, as they will have more flavor. Explore your area for the best places to get fresh produce. I use a local delivery service called Mike's Organic Delivery, and every week I get local, organic produce delivered to my door. I also shop at farmers' markets, where I get local artesian products such as nuts, nut butters, and dried fruits. Nature is already perfect; fresh, natural foods need little intervention to be flavorful.

Why Eat Plant-Based Foods?

We live in a world full of toxins: from the water we drink, to the air we breathe, to the fast-paced lives we keep. Unhealthy, processed foods are abundant, and many of us are sick, overweight, tired, stressed out, or on multiple medications. Our children are obese and spend much of their time inside playing computer games, watching TV, and sitting around. We lack fresh air, nature, creativity, fun, and community in our lives. We spend countless hours glued to our cell phones, computers, and iPads—we live in a world overrun by technology.

A diet that consists largely of sugar, dairy, fast food, flour products, coffee, sodas, alcohol, chemical additives, GMO grains, food preservatives, and drugs, among other things—the standard American diet—can cause the body to become too acidic. When your body is too acidic, you get sick. Eliminating these products is key to living a healthy life. We are the only species on this planet that eats cooked, processed foods. Wild animals, big and small, eat raw, fresh foods. These raw foods have enzymes that our high-sugar, processed foods lack. Animals are active, breathe fresh air, and get plenty of sunlight. We need to go back to the beginning, back to when we used to eat fresh, real food.

Many people feel that adopting a raw, plant-based diet is expensive. While this may be true, good food will keep you healthy. Spend more on healthy, whole foods now so you won't have to spend that money on hospital bills later. Your health and the health of your family members is the best investment you can make, and there are many ways to make healthy eating more affordable (e.g., buy food in bulk, plant your own herbs and vegetables, sign up for a co-op). Eating a nutritious, raw, organic, plant-based diet will keep you happy, healthy, energized, and looking and feeling young.

What is Art?

For me, art is life—we are all artists. How we dress, decorate our rooms, and, yes, make our food are forms of art. Creativity is one of the most important ways in which we express ourselves. I am an artist, painter, art educator, and self-taught chef who is inspired by Mother Nature, and especially by the seasons. I thrive in that beautiful space where the imagination has no limits and colors and shapes come alive.

I love teaching art classes and cooking classes. When I teach art to my students, we have so much fun. They inspire me, and I inspire them—it's a constant flow of energy. Being an artist means allowing yourself to enjoy the process without worrying so much about the destination. The older we get, the more perfect we want everything to be. When teaching, I often hear "I can't draw," "I can't paint," "I can't cook," "I'm not a good artist," or "I'm not creative" from various students, and my answer is always the same: "Just have fun!" Allow your inner child to play and let go of judgment and expectations. When you find yourself in this blissful state, you will create magic.

Art, like life, can be messy at times. We are always in the process of learning and discovering new things. Don't be afraid to get your hands dirty—you will clean it up at the end. Start creating, experimenting, and having fun in your kitchen, and create your own raw food art.

Tips for Getting Healthy

A simple diet that includes plenty of fresh water, greens, vegetables, fruits, nuts, and seeds means vitality, longevity, good health, shiny hair, beautiful skin, and lots of energy. Here are some simple things you can do to improve your health and well-being:

- Drink plenty of fresh water.
- Install a filtration system in your home to avoid fluoride and chlorine contaminating your food and water.
- Avoid GMO foods, processed foods, and fast foods.
- Eat organic to avoid ingesting harmful pesticides and chemicals that are sprayed on nonorganic food.
- When cooking, use oils, table salt, white sugar, and processed seasonings sparingly. Choose fresh herbs, pink Himalayan crystal salt or Celtic sea salt, and spices to flavor your food instead.
- Chew your food! Many people rush through their meals and don't chew food properly.
- Exercise not just at the gym but outdoors (e.g., hike, walk, run, ride a bike, or swim in the ocean or sea).
- Spend as much time outside as you can, no matter what season it is.
- Use natural beauty products (e.g., makeup, body care) and avoid products made with chemicals.
- Use all-natural cleaning products in your home. Many traditional cleaners have chemicals that are harmful to our health.
- Avoid plastic as much as possible. Store your food in glass or stainless steel containers instead.
- Don't use a microwave to prepare food, as it can destroy vital nutrients.
- Keep a food journal and write down everything you eat for six to eight weeks. Also be sure to record how you feel after eating. You may see that some foods, such as dairy or meat, for example, make you tired, give you a headache, or make your stomach upset. Look for patterns. Many people have food sensitivities and are not even aware of it.
- Try to cook food at home as much as possible and save your meals out for special occasions.

- Plant a garden or join a community garden.
- Start cooking homemade meals for your friends and family.
- Introduce lots of raw food into your daily routine (e.g., an easy green smoothie or juice in the morning, a salad for lunch, and fruit for a healthy snack on the go).
- Get familiar with your local farms, health food stores, and community. Together, you can build something great in your neighborhood.
- Avoid coffee, alcohol, and cigarettes.
- Join a yoga and/or meditation class.
- Watch sunrises and sunsets. Take your shoes off and feel connected to the earth.
- Turn off your Wi-Fi occasionally and enjoy your time uninterrupted by technology.
- Rotate your food so you are eating different foods every day.
- Think like an animal. Before you buy or eat something, ask, "Would a lion, cow, or duck eat this?" Every piece of food you decide to ingest can bring health or sickness—the choice is yours.
- Establish a connection with your food. Look at the beautiful colors and shapes, and let them inspire you.

- Be grateful for the life you live. Remember: you are in charge of your life. Love, give, and inspire and share "life's goodies" with others. What you give will come back to you multiplied.
- Be love. See with the eyes of love. Hear messages of love. Spread love.
- Bless your food and thank it for nourishing your body.

Making Food Colorful

My recipes are very colorful, as you'll see throughout this book. Here are some quick tips for achieving rainbow-colored recipes using natural ingredients:

- Red: beets (or beet powder), goji berries, cranberries, raspberries, cherries, watermelon, strawberries, or hibiscus tea
- Orange: carrots (or carrot powder), sweet potatoes, oranges, or pumpkins. You can also create an orange color by mixing red and yellow foods/ingredients.
- Yellow: pineapple, mangos, corn, or turmeric powder
- Green: spinach, avocado, spirulina, chlorella, wheatgrass, moringa, or green matcha powder. You can also create a green color by mixing blue and yellow foods/ingredients.
- Blue: Blue coloring is the hardest to make. Yes, blueberries are blue, but when you mix them, you will get a purple color. To achieve a great blue color, I use E3Live Blue Majik powder or Thai Butterfly Pea Blue Flower tea.
- Purple: purple cabbage, beetroot powder, purple grapes, blueberries, blackberries, or maqui berry powder. You can also create a purple color by mixing red and blue foods/ingredients.
- White: For a white color, or to make colors lighter, use coconut meat or shredded coconut, cashews, or bananas (e.g., mix white color with purple to make lavender or white color with red to make pink).

These are just some examples—the possibilities are endless. Mixing your own colors is like painting and inventing your own color palette. Just experiment. Remember that when you add something acidic like lime or lemon juice, your color will change, too.

Kitchen Tools and Ingredients

MAIN KITCHEN TOOLS

People spend so much money on cars, tropical vacations, designer clothes, and dining at fancy restaurants when they could be investing in their health instead. Investing in your health is true wealth. Research and purchase good-quality kitchen appliances to help you easily prepare healthy recipes at home. I will discuss some of the most important kitchen tools in the following section. Remember that you don't necessarily need to purchase the exact tools I use in this book—other products will work just fine, although results might vary slightly. Choose the products that work best with your budget, cooking goals, and kitchen space.

JUICER

Juicing is a process that extracts water and nutrients from produce (e.g., veggies, greens, and fruits) and separates the fiber, or juice pulp. Without the fiber, your digestive system doesn't have to work as hard to break down the food and absorb the nutrients. Organic, freshly made green and vegetable juices are very powerful and healing. Make sure you drink lots of green juices and not just fruit juices.

There are many types of juicers, and I will discuss a few here. They are all great, and the one you choose will depend on your individual needs and budget. Do some research to see which type will work best for you. I have a few juicers, but I love my Angel juicer.

- Centrifugal juicer: This type is the least expensive; it is fast and easy to clean, but the heat can quickly destroy the nutrients in a juice, so you should drink the juice made in a centrifugal juicer right away.
- Cold press juicer: There are a couple types of cold press juicers. First, is a mastication juicer, which is a juicer with a single gear. Making juice at a lower speed is better since there is very little heat created, and heat causes oxidation. Second, is a twin gear juicer. This type of juicer operates on a very slow speed, which means no heat or oxidation.
- Hydraulic press juicer: This type of juicer is very expensive but top-of-the-line. It does not require the use of heat or electricity, so the juice is very rich and nutritious but takes longer to make.
- Manual juicers: There are two main types of manual juicers: one that is commonly used for wheatgrass, leafy greens or vegetables, and one that is primarily used to juice citrus fruits.

BLENDER

Investing in a good-quality blender is very important because you'll be using your high-speed blender the most while preparing raw foods. I love my Vitamix, and I use it many times a day to make smoothies, desserts, and raw soups, among other things. If you can afford to invest in a Vitamix, I recommend it. Otherwise, many other companies make great high-speed blenders (e.g., Blendtec, Cuisinart, Omega, and Breville). Make sure, as with your juicer, that you purchase one that is fast but gentler on your produce.

FOOD PROCESSOR

A good-quality food processor is a necessity for any chef. I use mine to make cakes, desserts, and ice cream, as well as to chop veggies, and I can't imagine my life without it! You can use the Vitamix for some of these tasks, but for some recipes you'll need a good processor, too. It'll cost you a few pennies, but believe me when I say it's a worthy investment. A good food processor will last you for years. My food processor of choice is a Cuisinart food processor. I have a professional one, and it's amazing. I also have a mini food processor, but it's essentially only good for chopping: the motor and bowl capacity won't allow you to do much else.

DEHYDRATOR

A dehydrator uses low temperatures and a fan to dry food. The dehydration process allows you to prepare/cook food without destroying the food's life force. You can use it to make desserts, cookies, crackers, wraps, chips, pizza, pasta, and many other raw dishes. A dehydrator can also be used to warm up foods. There are many different types to choose from, and the one you choose will depend on your budget and how much space you have in your kitchen. I love my Excalibur dehydrator.

OTHER MISCELLANEOUS TOOLS

Here are several more helpful kitchen tools:
- Spiralizer: For making all kinds of raw pasta (e.g., from zucchini, cucumbers, sweet potatoes, and more).
- Mandolin: For slicing vegetables thinly.
- Coconut opener: For opening young Thai coconuts. I have a Coco Jack, and I find it to be the easiest to use, but there are many other options out there.
- Cutting board: I prefer a glass or wooden one, but there are many kinds available and all will work just fine.
- Mason jars: To store your juices, smoothies, and other foods such as dry nuts and beans.

They come in many shapes, colors, and sizes.

- Mixing bowls: I prefer bowls made from glass, stainless steel, or porcelain. I try to avoid plastic, but plastic may be the best option for those who have kids.
- Sharp knives: Invest in good knives. Stainless steel or ceramic knives are excellent.
- Peeler: Good to have for peeling nonorganic produce.
- Scrub brush: Great for scrubbing potatoes, carrots, and other veggies.
- Strainers and colanders: Available in stainless steel or plastic. Helpful for rinsing fruits and greens.
- Dishes: I collect colorful, handmade dishes from around the world. Your choice of dinnerware can greatly influence your presentation of a dish, so have fun with it and choose something that allows your personality to shine!
- Ice cream maker: There are many to choose from, depending on your budget.
- Nut milk bag: For making milk and cheese from nuts.

OLENKO'S FAVORITE COOKING INGREDIENTS

- Salts: Pink Himalayan crystal salt and Celtic sea salt
- Natural sweeteners: Lucuma powder, mesquite powder, dates, maple syrup, coconut sugar, and coconut nectar. Unsulphured dried fruits (e.g., apricots, cherries, or figs) can also be used as natural sweeteners.
- Sour taste: Lemon juice, lime juice, raw apple cider vinegar, and raw coconut vinegar
- Creamy textures: Coconut meat from Thai coconuts or Jamaican coconuts, cashews, macadamia nuts, raw coconut butter, ripe bananas, or sun-dried tomatoes
- Cheesy: Nutritional yeast
- Oils: Coconut oil, chia seed oil, hemp seed oil, and flaxseed oil. These oils are great to use in salad dressings or to add a little flavor to your dish. I also use coconut oil, along with cacao butter and coconut butter, in my raw chocolates.
- Essential oils: Peppermint, lemon, lavender, and orange. My favorite company is Young Living. When using essential oils, make sure they are high quality and made for internal use. You only need a drop or two; otherwise, they may overpower your dish.
- Fruity flavor: Jackfruit, durian, mango, berries, apples, and persimmons
- Dried fruits: Mulberries, figs, and dates (look for unsulphured)
- Spices: Turmeric or curry powder, cayenne pepper, Ceylon cinnamon, vanilla (I love the vanilla flavor by Medicine Flower), clove, ginger, and cardamom
- Chocolate: Use raw cacao powder, not cocoa powder. You can also use carob powder.
- Seeds: Chia, hemp, pumpkin, sunflower, and buckwheat groats
- Nuts: Walnuts, pecans, hazelnuts, macadamia nuts, Brazil nuts, cashews, and pistachios
- Superfoods: Maca, lucuma, and mesquite powders, and medicinal mushrooms such as reishi or chaga

You Are Love

Your purpose is to live your life in joy.

We didn't come here to struggle or suffer.
We came here to find love
To see the light
To spread kindness and compassion
To feel good
To eat well
To sleep well
To live in harmony
To live our lives in joy.

Appreciate your life.
Breathe,
and with each breath feel joy.
Be grateful and thankful for everything and everyone.
Be nice
Smile
Be happy
Be healthy
Be yourself
Create
Love.

Nature is our mother.
Give thanks to Mother Earth for your food, air, beauty, and abundance of beautiful colors, shapes, smells, and flavors.
Spread love and compassion to all living beings,
as we are all part of one family, and this Planet Earth is our home.
Nature and plant medicine are here to serve us.
Nature heals us.

We search for peace outside, but only inner peace can heal.
Nothing will heal you unless you are willing to let go
To forget
To forgive
To love
To be in the light.

So love
Let go
Be more open
Don't judge
Forgive yourself and others.

You are here to
Love
Be happy
See beauty
Create a peaceful world and art.

Feeling joy is an important part of your life,
and this is why you came here.

You are pure positive energy
You are love
You are light

We are one

So it is

Namaste

26

Sunshine
Warm heart
Fresh air
Longer days
Green grass
Birds chirping
Flower blossoms
Butterflies
Bees
Spiders
Ants
Spring showers
Rainbows
Kisses
Breathe and just be

Spring

Watermelon Smoothie

Makes 2 smoothies

Ingredients:
1 small watermelon
Fresh mint or basil, to taste

I love spring—the warm days and sunshine—and what better way to celebrate spring than to have a picnic with friends or family in the park. Watermelon smoothies, raw oatmeal cookies (next page), and fresh fruits are easy to make and will keep you full for hours while you enjoy time in nature.

Instructions: Cut watermelon into cubes and process in a high-speed blender. Add mint or basil and mix again. Serve immediately or store for up to 24 hours in a mason jar in the fridge.

Oatmeal Cookies

Makes about 15–20 cookies

Ingredients:
2 tablespoons chia seeds
2 1/2 cups gluten-free oats
8 ripe bananas
3 tablespoons dried, unsulphured cherries
or raisins
1/2 teaspoon Ceylon cinnamon
Pinch of ginger powder

I have been making oatmeal muffins like this for years, and when I began my journey as a raw vegan, I decided to make my oatmeal muffins into raw cookies. My husband, Bill, and our friends say these are their absolute favorite cookies. I can't make enough of them! Make sure your bananas are very ripe and spotty so your cookies will be naturally sweet and delicious.

Instructions: Soak chia seeds in 1/2 cup filtered water for 10 minutes. Next, mix all other ingredients in a large bowl. Start by smashing the bananas with a fork, and then add the cherries, cinnamon, ginger, and soaked chia seeds. Mix until smooth and add the gluten-free oats last. For this recipe, I divided the batch into three bowls and made three kinds of cookies: plain banana cookies, raw chocolate cookies, and goji berry cookies. You can add nuts, shredded coconut, essential oils, dried fruits, or superfoods to create almost any flavor you want. For the raw chocolate cookies, I added 1 tablespoon raw cacao powder. For the goji berry cookies, I added 1/2 cup dried, unsulphured goji berries. These cookies get their sweetness from the bananas, so it is crucial that you use very ripe bananas. If you prefer an even sweeter flavor, add 1 tablespoon maple syrup or raw coconut nectar. When you are happy with your chosen flavor, use your hands to form cookies and place them on parchment paper or Teflon sheets. Dehydrate 5–6 hours at 115°F, and then flip cookies over and dehydrate until crisp, about another 2-3 hours. Store cookies in the fridge for up to 3-5 days or freeze them. They are great to use for raw ice cream sandwiches (see recipe on page 61). If you don't have a dehydrator, you can use muffin cups and bake them in the oven on 300°F for about 15–20 minutes, although they won't be considered raw.

Mini Strawberry Cheesecakes

Makes about 10-12 cheesecakes

Crust:
1 1/2 cups almonds or walnuts
1/2 cup pumpkin seeds
10 Medjool dates, pitted
1 cup dried, unsulphured
mulberries
1/2 lemon, juiced
Pinch of cardamom
Pinch of Ceylon cinnamon

Filling:
3 cups raw cashews or macadamia nuts
(soaked in filtered water
for 1 hour)
1/2 cup fresh-squeezed lemon
or lime juice
1 tablespoon maple syrup (or more if you
prefer a sweeter dessert)
2 very ripe bananas
1 tablespoon vanilla extract
Pinch of Celtic sea salt
1 cup strawberries

Topping:
1 cup strawberries, cut in halves

These raw/no-bake cheesecakes are the perfect healthy dessert. You can bring them to a party or family gathering, or just enjoy them at home. Substitute strawberries with other seasonal fruits, like peaches, blueberries, or raspberries.

Instructions: Soak nuts for filling and set aside for 1 hour. Then, place all ingredients for the crust in a food processor. Process until you have a sticky, dough-like consistency. Take a small amount of the crust mixture and press into the bottom of muffin tins or mini cheesecake dishes. Next, mix all filling ingredients except the strawberries in a clean food processor or high-speed blender. Process until smooth. Layer the filling on top of the crust (use about half of the filling mixture). Add strawberries to the remaining filling mixture and mix again—it will turn a nice pink color. Pour the pink layer on top of each mini cheesecake. Place in the freezer for about three hours or until they are set. Serve with fresh strawberries on top. If you choose to make one large cheesecake instead, it will need a bit longer to set.

Coconut Yogurt Parfait

Serves 3–4

Ingredients:
Meat of 2 young Thai coconuts
(about 2 cups)
1/2 cup coconut water
1 teaspoon vegan probiotic

Toppings:
Fresh berries
Fresh mint
Pumpkin seeds
Mulberries
Raw buckwheat groats

To Make Vanilla Yogurt:
1 tablespoon maple syrup
or raw coconut nectar
1–2 teaspoons fresh-squeezed
lemon juice
1 teaspoon vanilla extract

This raw yogurt parfait makes a great dessert or healthy breakfast.

Instructions: Carefully open your coconuts. I like to use the Coco Jack tool; it makes the whole process so easy. Once you've opened your coconuts, place all ingredients in a high-speed blender and blend until completely smooth and creamy. Transfer the mixture into a glass container and cover with cheesecloth, and then let it sit at room temperature for about 4–5 hours (allowing the probiotic culture to multiply). At this point, you will have plain yogurt. Store in the fridge and enjoy for up to 3 days. To make a parfait, add fresh berries, fresh mint, pumpkin seeds, mulberries, and raw buckwheat groats for extra crunch.

Additional Option: Make different yogurt flavors by adding fruits like strawberries or blueberries, or raw cacao powder to the plain yogurt and mixing in a high-speed blender. The possibilities are endless. Just have fun and experiment!

Raw Zucchini Pasta & Pesto Sauce

Serves 2-4

Pasta:
2-3 medium zucchini

Pesto Sauce:
1 cup baby spinach or kale
1/2 cup raw cashews or almonds
1 lemon, juiced
1 bunch of basil
1 cup filtered water
Pinch of pink Himalayan crystal salt
1 cup arugula
1/2 cup pignoli nuts
1 bunch of parsley
1-2 cloves garlic
Pinch of cayenne pepper

Topping:
2 carrots, shredded
1/2 cup purple cabbage

This light zucchini pasta is perfect for lunch or dinner. It looks like real pasta and tastes delicious. You can enjoy it at home or pack it in a glass container for a picnic in the park or for a hike.

Instructions: Run zucchini through a spiral pasta maker (e.g., Spirooli). Next, in a high-speed blender, mix everything for the pesto sauce. Pour the sauce over the pasta and top it off with carrots, purple cabbage, and fresh parsley. Serve immediately.

Additional Option: You can add raw olives or baby tomatoes as a topping (not shown in the photo) or sprinkle some nutritional yeast on top and garnish with edible flowers like marigolds and pansies.

Oatmeal Chocolate Bars

Makes about 16–18 bars

Oatmeal:
2 cups gluten-free oats
6 large, ripe bananas
1/2 cup unsulphured raisins
1/2 cup dried, unsulphured cherries
1/2 cup dried, unsulphured mulberries
1/3 cup sunflower seeds
1 teaspoon fresh-squeezed lemon juice
1/2 teaspoon Ceylon cinnamon
3 tablespoons coconut, shredded
2 tablespoons maple syrup
Pinch of ginger powder

Raw Chocolate:
1 cup raw cacao butter
5 tablespoons coconut oil
1 1/2 cups raw cacao powder
3 tablespoons date sugar
2-3 tablespoons maple syrup
1 tablespoon maca powder
1/4 teaspoon Celtic sea salt
Pinch of cayenne pepper
1/2 teaspoon medicinal vanilla or vanilla extract
2 tablespoons lucuma powder

Raw chocolate + oats + bananas + dried fruits = perfection. These bars are delicious—great for kids and chocolate lovers alike.

Instructions: Mix all oatmeal ingredients in a large bowl. Start by smashing the bananas with a fork, and then slowly add the rest of the ingredients, mixing until well combined and sticky. Next, line a medium-size, shallow glass dish with parchment paper and spread mixture out on top of paper. A brownie dish will work great, too. Using a spoon or fork, press the mixture into the bottom of the dish. Next, prepare the raw chocolate layer.

Raw Chocolate: Melt cacao butter and coconut oil on very low heat, about 95–105°F. Use a double boiler so you can temper the chocolate. Add cacao powder and mix slowly with a wooden spoon. Next, add the rest of the ingredients and keep mixing until perfectly smooth. Pour mixture over the oatmeal. Sprinkle some raw cacao nibs, sea salt, and cinnamon on top for added texture. Put in the freezer to set and cut as desired. Store the bars in the freezer in a glass container.

Carrot Cake

Serves about 10

Carrot Cake:
3 cups carrots, chopped
1 cup walnuts
1 cup Medjool dates, pitted
1 teaspoon Ceylon cinnamon
2 tablespoons raw buckwheat groats
1/3 cup dried, unsulphured mulberries

Cashew Frosting:
2 cups cashews (soaked in filtered water for 30–45 minutes)
1 ripe banana
1/2 cup raw coconut water or filtered water
1-2 tablespoons maple syrup (or more if you prefer a sweeter dessert)

When I think of spring, I think of bunnies and carrots. This recipe is all about celebrating love, light, springtime, and new beginnings.

Instructions: Soak 2 cups cashews for frosting before beginning the cake base. Set aside. Then, in a food processor, mix carrots, walnuts, dates, and cinnamon until well combined. Sprinkle buckwheat groats and mulberries into the bottom of a cake dish, and then layer about two-thirds of the carrot cake base on top and spread evenly. Set the rest of the mixture aside for the top and prepare frosting.

Drain cashews (after they have soaked), and then mix all ingredients in a high-speed blender until smooth. Pour half of the mixture on top of the carrot cake base and press with a fork or spoon until smooth. Next, add another layer of carrot cake base, and then finish up with the top layer of cashew frosting. For a sweeter cake, sprinkle more dried mulberries between the layers. Allow cake to set in the freezer for about 4 hours or overnight. When ready to serve, sprinkle some shredded coconut on top, decorate with spring flowers, and enjoy.

Arugula Salad with Blue Cheese

Serves 1-2

Salad:
2 cups baby arugula
1 cup baby spinach
1 cup baby beet leaves
1/2 cup raw or sprouted garbanzo beans
1 pear, sliced
1 cup red grapes
1 cup Brussels sprouts, shredded
5-6 pieces green asparagus

Dressing:
3 tablespoons raw apple cider vinegar
1/2 lemon, juiced
2 tablespoons chia seed oil
or hemp seed oil
Pinch of cayenne pepper
1/2 teaspoon nutritional yeast

I love this light, spring salad. The greens, pears, grapes, and raw cheese are the perfect combination. Enjoy as a light meal or appetizer.

Instructions: Arrange your greens in a salad bowl, and then add Brussels sprouts, asparagus, grapes, pear, and garbanzo beans. Top with blue cheese and dressing. Add edible spring flowers like pansies or dandelions for additional color.

Blue Cheese: Follow **Macadamia Cheese** recipe on page 140.

Broccoli Soup

Serves 1-2

Soup:
2 cups broccoli
1 1/2 cup filtered water
1 clove garlic
1/2 teaspoon pink Himalayan crystal salt
Pinch of cayenne pepper
1/2 teaspoon nutritional yeast
1/2 teaspoon curry powder

Cream:
1/2 cup filtered water
1/2 cup sun-dried tomatoes
1 cup baby tomatoes
1/2 lemon, juiced
1 Medjool date
1/2 cup raw macadamia nuts
1/4 teaspoon Celtic sea salt

This is a perfect, light, and healthy spring soup that you can enjoy at home, or put it in a Mason jar and bring it to work, park or wherever you go. Broccoli is my favorite vegetable, and it's like my own little superhero. Broccoli has so many, health benefits. It is low in calories and rich in essential vitamins and minerals. Broccoli is a good carb and is high in fiber too.

Instructions: In a high-speed blender, mix soup and cream ingredients separately, and then arrange on the plate. Garnish with nutritional yeast, cayenne pepper, sunflower sprouts, baby tomatoes, and edible flowers. This soup is easy to make and is perfect for lunch or as an appetizer on a spring day.

Mini Juice Detox

Each juice serves 1–2

Green Awakening:
5–6 kale leaves
1 green apple
1 small zucchini
1 inch ginger
1 lemon (with peel)
1/2 cup cilantro

Balancing Glow:
3–4 medium carrots
1 green apple
1 orange
2 large tomatoes
1 large red pepper
1/2 lemon (with peel)
1 inch fresh turmeric (or turmeric powder)

Red Harmony:
3 tomatoes
1 apple
1 red pepper
1 lemon (with peel)
2 red beets

Burgundy Well-Being:
2 cups baby kale
2 cups baby spinach
1 zucchini
1 lemon (with peel)
1 inch ginger
3 beets
1/2 pineapple (without the skin)

A juice fast for 1–3 days is a perfect way to clean up your system. On a day you are fasting, drink plenty of fresh juices—at least three liters. Drink lots of water, fresh coconut water, and herbal tea. If you feel tired, rest, take a nap, enjoy a relaxing bath with essential oils, go for a walk, or listen to some soothing music. The best time to do a juice fast is over the weekend when you are home and can rest.

Instructions: Use a juicer for your mini juice detox. The amount of juice you'll get will depend on your juicer. To make each juice, press each ingredient through your juicer, one at a time, and then shake together and serve.

Purple Magic:
1 lemon (with peel)
4 cups purple cabbage
1 apple
1 pear

Hello Yellow:
5 oranges
2 carrots
1/2 pineapple (without the skin)
1/2 lime (with peel)
1/2 lemon (with peel)

Chocolate Bars

Makes about 15 bars, depending on size

Ingredients:
1 cup raw cacao butter
5 tablespoons coconut oil
1 1/2 cup raw cacao powder (or more if you prefer darker chocolate)
5-6 tablespoons maple syrup or date sugar
1/8 teaspoon pink Himalayan crystal salt
1/2 teaspoon medicinal vanilla or vanilla extract or powder

If you love chocolate, this recipe is for you. I truly believe that in order to make smooth, velvety, and mouthwatering chocolate, you need to add a bit of love. While mixing chocolate, make sure your emotions are positive and you think of joy, happiness, passion, love, friends, and good health. All these emotions will be imprinted in your chocolate.

Instructions: Melt cacao butter and coconut oil on very low heat, about 105°F. Use a double boiler so you can temper the chocolate. Add cacao powder and mix slowly with a wooden spoon. Next, add the rest of the ingredients and keep mixing until perfectly smooth. You can add superfoods like chaga and reishi mushrooms, lucuma or maca powder, dried rose petals, nuts, seeds, dried fruits, or a drop or two of good-quality essential oils. For a mold, I used a brownie dish, but you can use any molds you like.

For the toppings, I used goji berries, shredded coconut, walnuts, hazelnuts, and chia seeds, but the possibilities are endless. Choose toppings that have fun colors and textures. Place chocolates in the fridge to set and then pop them out of the molds and store in the fridge or freezer for up to 12 weeks in a tightly sealed glass container.

Maki Roll

Serves 1-2

Rolls:
2 raw nori sheets
1/4 red pepper
1/4 yellow pepper
1/2 avocado
Few slices cucumber
Small carrot
Fresh parsley and chives

Orange-Mango Sauce:
1 orange
1/2 mango
1–2 inches fresh ginger

Maki rolls are perfect as a light lunch or fun appetizer to bring to a party or family gathering.

Instructions: Using a sharp knife, slice the vegetables lengthwise into long, thin pieces. Roll the nori sheets into cone shapes and wet the seams so the rolls stay together. Stuff the roll with the sliced vegetables and arrange as desired.

Orange-Mango Sauce: Peel the orange, mango, and ginger, and place into a high-speed blender. Blend until smooth and serve on the side.

Additional Option: For a healthy, raw alternative to soy sauce, use raw coconut aminos made by Coconut Secret.

Pink Jicama Salad

Serves 1–2

Salad:
1 cup fresh Jicama, cut in long strips
1 cup purple cabbage, chopped
1 ripe mango, sliced
1 lemon, juiced
Pinch of Celtic sea salt
2 cups carrots, shredded
2 tablespoons dried, unsulphured mulberries
1 banana, cubed
Sesame leaves or lettuce

Mango Sauce:
1 ripe mango
1/2 carrot
2 Medjool dates
3 tablespoons filtered water
1 teaspoon hemp seed oil
Fresh herbs (cilantro and mint work well)

Enjoy this beautiful pink salad as a light lunch, side dish, or appetizer to share with your family and friends. The white jicama will change to a beautiful pink color after you add purple cabbage to the mix. Pure magic.

Instructions: Mix all salad ingredients in a bowl. Serve on sesame leaves or lettuce.

Mango Sauce: Mix all sauce ingredients in a high-speed blender and serve with salad.

Pasta Italiana

Serves 4

Pasta:
4–5 medium zucchini

Red Sauce:
1 cup sun-dried tomatoes
3 tablespoons goji berries
1 cup fresh tomatoes
2 cloves garlic
1/3 cup fresh beets, cubed
Celtic sea salt (to taste)
Few pieces of fresh basil and parsley

White Sauce:
1 cup raw macadamia nuts
3/4 cup filtered water
1 teaspoon vegan probiotic
1/4 teaspoon pink Himalayan crystal salt
Pinch of black pepper
Pinch of chili pepper
1/3 teaspoon nutritional yeast
1 tablespoon lemon juice

This raw pasta dish is a perfect alternative to regular cooked pasta. It's flavorful, light, and so delicious. Simple, natural ingredients are best for our bodies—just like Mother Nature intended.

Pasta: Run zucchini through a spiral pasta maker (e.g., Spirooli).

Red Sauce: Soak sun-dried tomatoes in water for 30 minutes and then use 3 tablespoons of water from the sun-dried tomatoes. Process with all other red sauce ingredients in a food processor or high-speed blender.

White Sauce: Mix all white sauce ingredients in a high-speed blender.

Presentation: Serve your red and white sauces over your raw pasta and garnish with fresh baby tomatoes, basil, and sweet pea shoots. You can add other chopped veggies (e.g., raw peppers, cucumbers, broccoli, olives, or cauliflower) on top of your pasta. Just have fun with it and try something new.

Garden Dip Crackers

Serves 4

Crackers:

2 1/2 cups buckwheat groats, sprouted
(see instructions on page 68)
1 cup flaxseed
1 large onion
3 cloves garlic
1 1/2 cups fresh tomatoes
1/2 cup carrots, chopped
Pinch of cayenne pepper
1 tablespoon lemon juice
Celtic sea salt, to taste
1 tablespoon za'atar spice (mix of sumac,
thyme, sesame seeds, hyssop,
and oregano)
8 leaves of fresh basil
Pinch of black pepper

Spring Veggie Dip:

6 cups baby spinach (you can use romaine
lettuce or arugula, too), chopped
1 small red onion, chopped
1 teaspoon Celtic sea salt
1 teaspoon za'atar spice
1/2 teaspoon cumin
2 cloves garlic
10 Israeli artichokes (about 1 cup),
washed and chopped
Pinch of Aleppo pepper
1 tablespoon nutritional yeast
1 lemon, juiced
1 green pepper, chopped
1 cup nuts (I used Macadamia nuts, but
you can use walnuts or cashews, too)

These crackers are raw, gluten free, and easy to make. Enjoy them as a snack or appetizer with my Spring Veggie Dip.

Instructions: For oil-free crackers, mix all cracker ingredients in a food processor (if you want, add 1 teaspoon of liquid coconut oil for a different texture). If you'd like to make several flavors from your batch, divide the mixture into 2 or 3 batches and add different toppings to each. Using a spatula, spread the mixture(s) onto Teflon sheets. Sprinkle toppings such as dried onion, garlic powder, dried herbs (e.g., thyme, tarragon, oregano, rosemary), black or white sesame seeds, hemp seeds, pumpkin seeds, or nuts—whatever you happen to have in your kitchen. Place in dehydrator for about 5–8 hours at 110°F (or longer, depending on how soft or dry you like your crackers). Cut into desired shapes. I made mine into small squares and very dry for my dip. You can also make pizza dough like this.

Spring Veggie Dip: Place nuts in a high-speed blender and cover with filtered water, about one cup. Once processed, transfer to a large bowl and mix with veggies, spices, spinach, and the rest of the ingredients. Serve over crackers or with veggies on the side (e.g., sliced zucchini, baby tomatoes, fresh basil leaves, sliced cucumber, carrots, beets, broccoli, radishes, celery, or Brussels sprouts).

Ice Cream Sandwiches

Serves 7–8

Raw Chia Banana Cookies:
6 large, ripe bananas
1/3 cup sunflower seeds
Pinch of Ceylon cinnamon
1/2 lemon, juiced
1–2 tablespoons maple syrup
or raw coconut nectar
4 tablespoons chia seeds (soaked in 1/2
cup filtered water for 10 minutes)

Ice Cream Filling:
10 large, ripe bananas, frozen
2–3 Medjool dates, pitted
1 tablespoon coconut, shredded
Vanilla extract, to taste
1 small piece of red beet, for color
1 cup frozen or fresh raspberries
1 cup frozen or fresh blueberries
Pinch of Blue Majik powder

These yummy, sweet, refreshing, colorful ice cream sandwiches are great as a healthy snack for kids (and adults, too!).

Raw Chia Banana Cookies: Start by smashing the bananas with a fork, then add the rest of the ingredients, including the soaked chia seeds (when ready). Form cookies with your hands and place them on parchment paper or Teflon sheets. Dehydrate for 5–6 hours at 115°F, and then flip cookies over and dehydrate until crisp, about another 2–3 hours. Store cookies in the fridge for up to 3–5 days or freeze them. If you don't have a dehydrator, you can bake the cookies on your oven's lowest setting for about 20 minutes.

Ice Cream Filling: Peel the bananas, cut them into pieces, and place them in a glass container in the freezer. After the bananas are frozen, place them in a food processor and blend; you may need to stop periodically to scrape the sides. (Blend them all at once if you're making one flavor, or in batches if you're making more than one flavor.) For this recipe, I made three flavors: banana-coconut, raspberry, and blueberry. For banana-coconut, add 1 pitted Medjool date, 1 tablespoon shredded coconut, and vanilla extract to taste. For raspberry, add 1 cup frozen or fresh raspberries and a small piece of red beet for color. For blueberry, add 1 cup frozen or fresh blueberries and a pinch of Blue Majik by E3Live for a more intense blue color. Be sure to rinse the food processor between batches.

Presentation: Take a cookie and spread a layer of filling on top. Then, place another cookie on top of the filling and, using a spoon, fill more ice cream to the edges of the cookie and smooth so it looks like an ice cream sandwich. Place sandwiches in the freezer to set for about 2–3 hours and enjoy.

7 Chakras Smoothie

Serves 1

Red:
1/2 cup pomegranate seeds
1/2 cup strawberries

Orange:
1 small orange
1/2 cup papaya
1/2 cup mango

Yellow:
1 cup mango

Green:
1 cup spinach
1 mango

Blue:
1 cup fresh coconut meat
1 pinch of Blue Majik powder

Purple:
1/3 cup blackberries
1/3 cup raspberries
2 tablespoons cashews

Violet:
1/2 cup blueberries
1 banana
1 tablespoon chia seeds

This smoothie is inspired by the colors of the seven chakras. These colors reflect the different frequencies and energy flow of each chakra. If someone's chakras are weak, it is beneficial to eat foods that are the color of that chakra.

Instructions: Mix each color separately in a high-speed blender and layer in a tall glass. You'll need to rinse the blender after each color.

- *Red is the color of the root chakra (first chakra): Safety, survival, grounding, nourishment from the Earth's energy, physical strength. Foods: beets, strawberries, cranberries, tomatoes, and red peppers.*
- *Orange is the color of the sacral chakra (second chakra): Emotions, creativity, joyfulness, happiness, sexuality. Foods: pumpkin, papaya, persimmons, and oranges.*
- *Yellow is the color of the solar plexus chakra (third chakra): Mental activities, intellect, clarity, optimism, personal power, will. Foods: pears, bananas, mangos, yellow peppers, and lemons.*
- *Green is the color of the heart chakra (fourth chakra): Love, integration, compassion, family, love for nature. Foods: kiwi, green vegetables and greens, cucumbers, green grapes, and green peppers.*
- *Blue is the color of the throat chakra (fifth chakra): Self-expression, beauty, expression of truth, creative expression, communication, art. Foods: blueberries, blackberries, and blue algae.*
- *Purple (or deep indigo blue) is the color of the third-eye chakra (sixth chakra): Intuition, extrasensory perception, inner wisdom. Foods: purple grapes, purple cabbage, plums, and berries.*
- *Violet or white is the color of the crown chakra (seventh chakra): The universe, connection with spirituality, consciousness. Foods: purple potatoes, purple cauliflower, lavender, maqui berries, and acai berries.*

Banana-Watermelon Cake

Serves 8–10

Cake Base:
3-4 tablespoons coconut, shredded
8-10 Medjool dates (about 1 cup)
1/2 cup walnuts

Filling:
3 cups watermelon, cubed
5 very large, ripe, frozen bananas
4 tablespoons raw coconut butter
1 cup frozen blackberries
1 cup frozen raspberries

This cake is very light, nut free, and made from fruits. Imagine an ice cream watermelon cake. Perfect for a birthday party or family celebration.

Cake Base: On the bottom of a medium-size springform cake dish, sprinkle 3-4 tablespoons shredded coconut so your cake won't stick. Next, in a food processor, mix Medjool dates (about 1 cup) and 1/2 cup walnuts. Spread the raw dough on the bottom of your cake dish.

Filling: Mix watermelon, bananas, and raw coconut butter in a high-speed blender and pour over cake base. Add blackberries and raspberries. Mix them into the cake. Place in freezer until frozen. Decorate with fresh figs, blueberries, and edible violet flowers.

Beet Soup

Serves 1-2

Soup Base:
2 large beets, cubed (about 2 cups)
1 small carrot, chopped
1/3 small onion
1 small apple
1/5 teaspoon pink Himalayan crystal salt
1/2 teaspoon nutritional yeast
Pinch of paprika or chili powder
Pinch of black pepper
3 cups filtered water

Cashew Cream:
1/2 cup filtered water
1/3 cup fresh coconut meat
or raw coconut butter
1/2 cup cashews

This soup is a powerful antioxidant potion. Beets are great for your bones, liver, kidneys, and pancreas. This soup is full of vitamins and minerals: high in immune-boosting vitamin C, B, fiber, and potassium.

Instructions: In a high-speed blender, mix soup and cream ingredients separately, then combine. Garnish with fresh herbs and serve with flaxseed crackers.

Flaxseed Crackers: Soak 1 cup flaxseeds in 1 cup filtered water for 30 minutes. Next, add pink Himalayan crystal salt, cayenne pepper, and cumin to taste. Your mixture should be thick. Spread mixture over large nori wraps on a Teflon sheet. Dehydrate for 5-7 hours at 110°F, and then flip over and dehydrate for another 2-3 hours, until completely dry.

Donuts

**Makes about 15–20 donuts,
depending on size**

Donuts:
2 cups raw buckwheat groats, sprouted*
1/4 teaspoon nutmeg
1/4 teaspoon ginger powder
1 cup gluten-free oats
(processed to make a flour)
1 1/2 teaspoons Ceylon cinnamon
2 tablespoons mesquite powder
1/4 teaspoon Celtic sea salt
1 teaspoon vanilla powder
1 apple, cubed
13 large Medjool dates
1 cup coconut, shredded (I used reduced
fat and finely shredded)
2 small, ripe bananas
3 tablespoons coconut butter
1 cup additional gluten-free oats
(unprocessed)

Chocolate Frosting:
4 tablespoons coconut oil
3 tablespoons maple syrup
1 teaspoon vanilla extract or powder
5 tablespoons raw cacao powder
2 tablespoons carob powder

If you love donuts, you are in for a treat. And who doesn't love donuts? These donuts are healthy, gluten free, raw, colorful, and most importantly they can be prepared in advance and stored in the freezer for weeks. Whenever you are in the mood for a donut, just take one out and enjoy as a healthy treat.

To Sprout Buckwheat: Rinse 1 cup raw buckwheat and place in a glass container. Cover with filtered water and soak for about 2–4 hours. Drain groats into a colander or strainer and rinse well. Continue to let drain for about 8–12 hours, or longer, depending on humidity and temperature.

Donuts: Mix all ingredients but coconut butter and unprocessed oats in the food processor; you will need to stop periodically to scrape the sides. If you prefer sweeter donuts, add more dates or some maple syrup. Next, add 3 tablespoons coconut butter and process, and then add 1 cup gluten-free oats and mix with spoon. Then, using your hands, form medium-size balls and make a hole in the middle of each donut ball with your finger. You can sprinkle extra oats or shredded coconut on top. Place donuts on a Teflon sheet and dehydrate at 115°F for about 5–7 hours, depending on how soft you like your donuts. Top with a layer of chocolate frosting (see below), and then sprinkle shredded coconut, goji berries, pistachios, or cacao nibs. To make donut glazes, melt coconut oil and add colored powders like matcha powder for green, goji powder for orange, and Blue Majik powder for blue.

Chocolate Frosting: Melt and mix all ingredients, and then drizzle over donuts. Store donuts in the fridge for up to 3–5 days or freeze for later.

Vacation
Relax and Just be
Search for a sunrise at the beach
Toes in the sand
Swimming
Long naps
Sunbaths
Blue sky
Ice cream
Watermelon
Summer storms and Humid air
Go to the farm
Berries
Peaches
Tomatoes
Sunflowers
Family Fun and Adventures

Summer

Fruit-Infused Water

Serves 4

Raspberry Basil:
1/2 cup raspberries
A few pieces of fresh basil
A few lemon slices (optional)

Cucumber Mint:
1 cup cucumbers, sliced
A few pieces of fresh mint
Fresh basil, oregano, or thyme (optional)

Mango Basil:
1 cup mango, cubed
A few pieces of fresh basil
A few lemon or orange slices (optional)

Blackberry Herb Tonic:
1 cup blackberries
A few pieces of fresh mint, basil,
and rosemary
Fresh blueberries and watermelon

Making fruit-infused water is fun and easy. These refreshing flavors will keep you hydrated on a hot summer day. They are perfect to take to the park, picnic, or beach, and kids will enjoy them, too.

Instructions: Simply fill up desired number of mason jars with fruits and herbs, and then add filtered water. Cover and keep in the fridge for a couple hours or overnight.

Additional Option: Try fresh, raw coconut water instead of filtered water. Strawberries, apples, watermelons, peaches, and plums are great options, too. Don't be afraid to experiment! Remember to stay hydrated and drink at least 6-8 glasses of water every day.

Lavender-Blueberry Smoothie

Serves 1

Ingredients:
1 cup fresh blueberries
1 ripe banana
1/2 cup cashews
2–3 Medjool dates
2 cups filtered water
2–3 drops of therapeutic-grade
lavender essential oil
Fresh mint

This smoothie is perfect for a quick summer dessert. It's easy to make, and the color is so beautiful!

Instructions: Blend all ingredients in a high-speed blender. Garnish with fresh blueberries and fresh mint.

Veggie Burger

Serves 10

Raw Buckwheat Buns:
2 cups raw buckwheat, sprouted
1 cup sun-dried tomatoes (soaked in
filtered water for 1 hour)
1 tablespoon coconut oil
1 clove garlic (or more if you like garlic)
Pinch of cayenne pepper
1 tablespoon onion powder
1 teaspoon pink Himalayan crystal salt
Sesame seeds, for garnish

Burger Patties:
3 medium carrots, chopped
(about 1 1/2 cups)
1 whole red pepper, chopped
1 purple onion, chopped
1 corncob (cut kernels from cob)
2 cloves garlic
1 cup pistachios
1/3 cup almonds
1 large tomato
4–5 leaves of fresh basil
4–5 pieces of fresh parsley
1/2 teaspoon raw apple cider vinegar
1 teaspoon pink Himalayan crystal salt
1/2 teaspoon Jamaican curry powder

Toppings:
1 medium Portobello mushroom cup
Cucumber, sliced
Red pepper, sliced
Romaine lettuce
Avocado, sliced
Baby tomatoes

This raw veggie burger consists of three parts: a raw veggie burger, toppings, and a raw buckwheat bun. The buns can be made in advance and stored in the fridge for up to a few days or in the freezer for later.

Raw Buckwheat Buns: Rinse your buckwheat and soak it in filtered water. Change the water every 5–6 hours. Your sprouted buckwheat should be ready in about 12 hours, depending on the temperature of your home. When sprouted, rinse well and drain. Place all ingredients except the sesame seeds in a food processor, making sure to use only the tomatoes, not the water. Process until you've achieved a dough-like consistency. Then, using a spoon, create bun shapes with the dough. Sprinkle sesame seeds on top, if desired. Place buns on a Teflon sheet and dehydrate at 110°F for about 5–6 hours, flipping buns over halfway through. Watch that they don't become too dry or they will have more of a cracker-like texture. Store in the fridge for a few days or freeze for later.

Burger Patties: Slice all veggies, and then place all ingredients in a food processor and pulse. You want to create a burger-like consistency, so don't overprocess. Using a large spoon and clean hands, create burger patties. Place patties on a Teflon sheet and dehydrate at 110°F for about 8–10 hours, depending on how crispy you like your burgers. Flip patties over halfway. If you don't have a dehydrator, you can make the buns and burgers in the oven. They won't be 100% raw, but they will still be good and healthy. Just put the oven on the lowest setting and bake for about 20–30 minutes. Store in the fridge for up to a few days or freeze for later.

Continued.....

Raw Ketchup & Raw Mayonnaise

Served as sides

Raw Ketchup:
1 medium-size tomato, chopped
1 cup sun-dried tomatoes (soaked in filtered water for 20 minutes)
2 tablespoons fresh-squeezed lemon juice
1/2 teaspoon Celtic sea salt
1 clove garlic
2 tablespoons goji berries (soaked in filtered water for 20 minutes)
4 Medjool dates
3 tablespoons raw Macadamia nuts or cashews
Pinch of black pepper

Raw Mayonnaise:
1 cup cashews or Macadamia nuts (soaked in filtered water for 1 hour)
1/2 cup raw cauliflower, chopped
1 teaspoon yellow mustard
1/4 teaspoon Celtic sea salt
2 tablespoons fresh-squeezed lemon juice
2 Medjool dates
3 tablespoons coconut oil, melted
2 tablespoons raw white tahini
1/3 cup filtered water

Raw Ketchup: Mix all ingredients in a high-speed blender. Slowly add some of the water from the sun-dried tomatoes, mixing until you achieve your desired consistency. You want the ketchup to be thick, not watery, so don't add too much water. Store in the fridge for up to a few days.

Raw Mayonnaise: Place all ingredients in a high-speed blender and puree until smooth and creamy. Store in the fridge for up to a few days.

To assemble your sandwich, start with 1 medium Portobello mushroom cup. Next, place a raw veggie burger on top and follow with the toppings. Top with a buckwheat bun. Garnish with avocado, baby tomatoes, and fresh herbs. Serve ketchup and mayonnaise on the side.

Durian Pudding

Serves 2-4

Ingredients:
3-4 cups raw or frozen durian
*1/2 cup raw coconut meat
or coconut cream*
*2/3 cup fresh coconut water
or filtered water*
3 ripe, frozen bananas
*4-5 Medjool dates (or more
if you prefer a sweeter dessert)*
*1/2 teaspoon medicinal vanilla
or vanilla extract*

This is the perfect light summer dessert. You can also use it over raw ice cream or other raw desserts.

Instructions: Carefully open your coconut and use the coconut water as a base for your pudding. Next, add most of your raw coconut meat (save some for a garnish). Then, carefully open your durian, scoop out the pieces, and remove the pits. Add durian, coconut, bananas, dates, and vanilla. Mix all ingredients in a high-speed blender until smooth. This tastes just like real vanilla pudding, and it is so healthy. If you've never had durian before, you may not like it at first—many say that it is an acquired taste. Serve immediately.

Additional Option: Sprinkle pieces of raw chocolate on top (see recipe page 53).

Chocolate Lover's Truffles

Serves 18–20

Ingredients:
2 cups raw cacao powder
(plus 1/2 cup for rolling the truffles)
2/3 cup coconut oil, melted
5 tablespoons raw coconut nectar
or maple syrup
4 tablespoons lucuma powder
2/3 cup coconut, shredded
2 tablespoons raw coconut butter (whole
coconut puree)
8 Medjool dates
1/2 teaspoon pink Himalayan crystal salt
Pinch of cayenne pepper
1 teaspoon medicinal vanilla
or vanilla extract

These truffles are very, very rich. You can add 2-3 drops of therapeutic-grade essential oils like peppermint or orange for different flavors.

Instructions: Mix all ingredients in a food processor. You may have to stop periodically to scrape the sides. Use an ice cream scoop to scoop the mixture out of the food processor. Then, with your hands, form small balls. Roll truffles in raw cacao powder. Store in the fridge or freezer in a glass container.

Strawberry Pasta

Serves 2–4

Pasta:
2 medium zucchini

Strawberry Sauce:
3 cups strawberries (2 cups for sauce and 1 cup for garnish)
1 ripe, frozen banana
4 Medjool dates, pitted
1/2 cup fresh coconut meat
1 tablespoon raw coconut butter
3 tablespoons raw coconut water or filtered water
Fresh basil, for garnish

This recipe is inspired by my favorite childhood Polish pasta dish. The difference is using raw zucchini pasta instead of cooked wheat pasta. For best results, use fresh strawberries or berries from a farmers' market. Enjoy as a dessert or a light summer meal.

Pasta: Run zucchini through a spiral pasta maker (e.g., Spirooli).

Strawberry Sauce: Mix all ingredients in a high-speed blender and serve over zucchini pasta. Garnish with fresh strawberries and basil.

Additional Option: This works very well with other seasonal berries, like blueberries or raspberries. If you want your sauce to be sweeter, just add more dates.

Ginger-Almond-Chocolate Crumble

Serves 20

Base:

2/3 cup gluten-free oats
2 cups almond meal
2 tablespoons ginger powder (if you prefer milder taste, use 1 tablespoon)
1 1/2 tablespoons Ceylon cinnamon
4-5 tablespoons raw coconut nectar or maple syrup
2 cups Medjool dates, pitted (about 17 large dates)

Chocolate:

2 cups raw cacao powder
1 cup coconut oil
4-5 tablespoons coconut nectar or maple syrup
2 tablespoons lucuma powder
1/2 teaspoon medicinal vanilla or vanilla extract
Pinch of pink Himalayan crystal salt
Pinch of cayenne pepper

If you love ginger and chocolate, this is the perfect dessert for you.

Base: Sprinkle oats on the bottom of a glass pan and cover evenly. Place almond meal, ginger, and 1 tablespoon cinnamon in a mixing bowl. Add coconut nectar and mix with a spoon until it becomes sticky, like a crumb cake. Put aside 2 tablespoons for the end. Place dates in a food processor, add 1/2 tablespoon cinnamon, and blend. Add date mixture to the almond mixture, and use clean hands to combine. Spread the mixture over the oats. Top with 1/2 teaspoon cinnamon and set aside. Make the raw chocolate layer next.

Instructions: In a glass pan, melt the coconut oil and slowly add the rest of the ingredients. Keep mixing until smooth. Pour over the crumb cake mix. Take the 2 tablespoons of crumb cake you set aside and sprinkle on top. You can sprinkle more oats, too. Freeze for about 2 hours. Remove from freezer and cut into squares. Store in the freezer for up to a few weeks in a glass container.

Chocolate-Orange Blossom Truffles

Serves 15

Ingredients:
1 cup raw cacao powder
(plus 1/4 cup for rolling the truffles)
1 cup almonds
1 tablespoon coconut oil, melted
4 tablespoons maple syrup
1/3 teaspoon Ceylon cinnamon
1/4 teaspoon ginger powder
1 tablespoon lucuma powder
2 tablespoons raw coconut butter
(whole coconut puree)
10 Medjool dates, pitted
1/5 teaspoon pink Himalayan crystal salt
1 tablespoon orange blossom water
1 teaspoon Caramel Medicine Flower
(optional)
3 tablespoons filtered water

This recipe yields very rich dark chocolate truffles with an almond-caramel flavor. They are not super-sweet, so if you prefer a sweeter dessert, just add more maple syrup.

Instructions: Mix all ingredients in a food processor. You may have to stop periodically to scrape the sides. Use an ice cream scoop to scoop the mixture out of the food processor. Then, form truffles with your hands. You can also roll the truffles in raw cacao powder or lucuma powder, if desired. Store in the fridge or freezer in a glass container.

Red Cabbage, Mango & Chia Parfait

Serves 2-4

Chia:
1/3 cup filtered water
2 tablespoons chia seeds

Purple Color:
1 cup red cabbage, chopped
4 ripe, frozen bananas
6 Medjool dates
1 cup fresh or frozen raspberries

Yellow Color:
5 ripe mangos

This light, refreshing parfait is perfect for a hot summer day, and it is so rich and colorful!

Chia: Soak chia seeds in water for about 15 minutes or until the mixture becomes thick.

Purple Color: Mix all ingredients in a high-speed blender, and then set aside.

Yellow Color: Rinse blender after mixing purple color, and then blend mangos and set aside.

Presentation: In martini glass, layer the chia, yellow, and purple mixtures as desired. Top with fresh berries, like raspberries and blueberries, and fresh mint.

Jicama Tacos

Serves 2

Ingredients:
1 medium-size jicama
2 cups jackfruit, pitted
1 cup papaya, cubed
1 cup mango, cubed
1/2 cup pomegranate seeds
2 oranges
1/2 cup blueberries
1/2 cup blackberries
1 banana
1 lime
A few leaves of Romaine lettuce
A few sweet pea shoots

These tacos are great for a summer breakfast, an appetizer, or a healthy snack.

Instructions: Peel skin off jicama and slice into thin pieces. Place the Romaine lettuce leaves on a tray and layer jicama on top. Next, cut the remaining fruit into desired shapes and place on top of the jicama. Sprinkle berries and pomegranate seeds on top of your tacos, and then garnish with sweet pea shoots. Squeeze fresh lime juice over the tacos and serve with oranges on the side.

Vanilla-Coconut Macaroons

Serves 15-18

Ingredients:
3 cups coconut, shredded
2 large ripe bananas, mashed
1/2 teaspoon medicinal vanilla
or vanilla extract
Pinch of pink Himalayan crystal salt
2-3 tablespoons maple syrup
or raw coconut nectar

I love, love, love coconuts! These macaroons are super light and are made from just a few simple ingredients.

Instructions: Mix all ingredients in a large bowl until well combined. Use clean hands to form balls. Place balls on a mesh sheet and dehydrate at 110°F for about 6–12 hours, depending on how crunchy you like your macaroons. Store in the fridge for up to a week or freeze for later.

Additional Option: If you want to make different flavors, you can add fresh lemon juice, essential oils like peppermint or lavender, raw cacao powder, or pureed raspberries or blueberries. The natural pigments in different fruits will create beautiful and fun colors. You can use beet juice for a pink color or matcha powder or spirulina for green.

Pomelo-Dragon Fruit Salad

Serves 1-2

Salad:
1 1/2 cups pomelo pieces
(reserve skin for a bowl)
1 cup dragon fruit
About 8–10 pieces of crunchy
Romaine lettuce
2 tablespoons sunflower seeds
1 tablespoon hemp seeds

Dressing:
1/4 cup cashews
1/4 cup sun-dried tomatoes
1 clove garlic
1 lemon, juiced
Pinch of Celtic sea salt and black pepper

Coconut-Turmeric Crackers:
2 cups raw coconut meat
(from young coconuts)
1-2 tablespoons raw coconut water
1/2 teaspoon pink Himalayan crystal salt
1/2 teaspoon turmeric powder
1/2 teaspoon fresh-squeezed lemon juice

You can enjoy this fruity, light, summer salad as a meal or appetizer. Plus, the Coconut-Turmeric Crackers can be made as wraps or crackers, depending on how long you dehydrate them.

Dressing: Mix all dressing ingredients in a high-speed blender.

Coconut-Turmeric Crackers: Process all cracker ingredients in a blender or food processor until it reaches a smooth, spreadable consistency. Spread coconut batter on dehydrator sheets or parchment paper. Place in dehydrator at 110°F and check every few hours. I wanted crunchy crackers, so I dehydrated them longer—about 8 hours. Once crackers are dry and solid on top, flip them over and dehydrate for a few more hours. I left mine in the dehydrator for 8 hours, flipped them, and dried them for another 2-3 hours. When ready, break crackers into pieces and serve with salad.

Presentation: Combine all salad ingredients and arrange in the reserved pomelo skin. Decorate with chopped carrots and dragon fruit. Serve dressing on the side.

Watermelon-Chia Soup

Serves 2–4

Ingredients:
1 small watermelon, cubed and chilled in the fridge
10 strawberries (about 2 cups)
2 ripe mangos
Fresh mint
5 tablespoons chia seeds (soaked in 1 cup filtered water for 20 minutes)

This is such a refreshing appetizer or snack on a hot summer day. You can eat it at room temperature or cold.

Instructions: Soak chia seeds. Next, cut watermelon in half and scoop out the fruit so you can use the rind as a bowl to serve the soup. Mix the watermelon and other fruits in a high-speed blender. You can add other fruits such as fresh papaya, pineapple, lemon, or peaches. When ready to serve, pour the watermelon soup into the watermelon bowl, add chia seeds, and enjoy.

Mango Stew

Serves 4

Pasta:
1 large cucumber
5 small zucchini

Sauce:
6 ripe mangos
1 clove garlic
1 avocado
3 cups spinach
Pinch of Celtic sea salt
Pinch of black pepper
Lemon juice (optional)

This is a great summer dish for lunch or dinner—light, fruity, and delicious.

Pasta: Run cucumber and zucchini through a spiral pasta maker (e.g., Spirooli).

Instructions: Process all ingredients in a high-speed blender. Pour sauce over your raw noodles and enjoy.

Additional Option: Add sliced bananas, pomegranates, or jackfruit for a different flavor and texture.

Lasagna

Serves 2–4

Noodles:
2–4 medium zucchini

Red Sauce:
1 cup sun-dried tomatoes
(soaked in filtered water for 2 hours)
4 tablespoons filtered water
4 tablespoons raw sunflower seeds
1/2 cup baby tomatoes
1 teaspoon cilantro
1/2 lemon, juiced
2 cloves garlic
Celtic sea salt, to taste

White Sauce:
1/3 cup cashews
1/3 cup fresh Jamaican coconut meat
1/3 cup filtered water
Celtic sea salt, to taste

Green Sauce:
1/2 cup zucchini, cubed
1 clove garlic
1 cup arugula
2 tablespoons filtered water
3 tablespoons pignoli nuts
Pinch of Celtic sea salt
3 teaspoons nutritional yeast

This raw lasagna is full of fresh summer flavors and will be a great addition to your summer BBQ or family gathering.

Instructions: Blend each sauce separately in a high-speed blender, rinsing the blender in between. Store sauces in separate glass containers. Cut zucchini lengthwise and layer between the sauces in a glass dish. For best results, prepare the night before enjoying so the zucchini will have time to soak up the flavors of the sauces. Enjoy as an individual meal or bring to a family gathering to share with loved ones.

Pad Thai with Kelp Noodles

Serves 1-2

Jungle Peanut Sauce:
5 tablespoons raw jungle peanuts
or walnuts
1/2 lemon, juiced
3 tablespoons filtered water
4 tablespoons raw coconut aminos
(healthy version of soy sauce)
Pinch of pink Himalayan crystal salt
1 teaspoon nutritional yeast
1 tablespoon shredded coconut
or raw coconut meat
1 clove garlic
A few pieces of fresh basil
1/2 inch fresh ginger

Kelp Noodle Salad:
1 carrot, shredded
1 cucumber, cubed
1 bunch of fresh cilantro, chopped
1/3 cup baby tomatoes
1/2 fresh green or red pepper,
cut as desired

When I visited Thailand, I was so inspired by all the wonderful, fresh flavors. I wanted to create something inspired by my trip, so I came up with this light, summer dish.

Noodles: For the noodles, you will need 1 package of raw kelp noodles (12oz/340g). Rinse the noodles in filtered water, drain, and place them in a large mixing bowl.

Jungle Peanut Sauce: Mix all ingredients in a high-speed blender. Add a little water if the sauce is too thick. Mix sauce with your kelp noodles and let marinate for 15 minutes or longer. Serve over greens.

Kelp Noodle Salad: Toss your salad with noodles. For additional flavor, top with fresh mint, hemp seeds, raw jungle peanuts (or other nuts), and slices of lime.

Additional Option: Try different variations of this recipe with red or white shredded cabbage, mushrooms, radishes, spinach, or arugula.

Ice Cream Cones

Serves 6

Cones:
8 large, very ripe bananas
1 lemon, juiced

Mango Ice Cream (Yellow):
2 ripe mangos
1/4 cup raw macadamia nuts
1/2 lemon, juiced

Avocado Ice Cream (Green):
2 ripe avocados
2 tablespoons maple syrup
1/2 ripe mango
1 cup baby spinach
Pinch of Celtic sea salt

Blue Majik Ice Cream (Blue):
2 cups raw coconut meat
1/3 cup macadamia nuts
1 tablespoon maple syrup
Pinch of Blue Majik powder

Berry Sorbet (Purple):
2 ripe peaches or 1 cup frozen peaches
1 cup fresh or frozen blackberries
1/2 cup cashews
(soaked in filtered water for 30 min)

Raspberry Sorbet (Red):
3 cups fresh or frozen raspberries
1 tablespoon fresh-squeezed lemon juice

Cherry-Vanilla (White):
4 very ripe, frozen bananas
2 dates, broken into pieces
1/2 cup frozen or fresh pitted cherries

These fun ice cream cones are colorful, refreshing, fruity, and flavorful, and summertime is a perfect time to enjoy them!

Cones: Process all ingredients in a high-speed blender until smooth. For different colors, add: beet powder for red, spirulina powder for green, Blue Majik powder for blue, turmeric powder for yellow, and acai powder for purple. You can also add fruits like raspberries or blueberries, spinach, or beets. Just experiment and have fun!

Spread your desired mixture onto a Teflon sheet and dehydrate at 110°F for about 4 hours, and then flip. After 30 minutes to 1 hour, form into cone shapes and use water to seal the seam. Dehydrate for about 2-4 more hours or until dry. Store in the fridge for up to a week or freeze for later.

Ice Cream or Sorbet: Use seasonal or frozen fruits and add veggies, nuts, superfoods, and/or dried fruits to create a rainbow of ice cream flavors.

Continued next page...

Mango Ice Cream: Mix all ingredients in a high-speed blender. You can process in an ice cream maker or store the mixture in a glass container and freeze.

Avocado Ice Cream: Mix all ingredients in a high-speed blender. Transfer mixture to a glass container and add 1-2 tablespoons raw cacao nibs. Seal and freeze.

Berry Sorbet: Soak cashews. After 30 minutes, mix all ingredients in a high-speed blender. You can process in an ice cream maker or store the mixture in a glass container and freeze.

Blue Majik Ice Cream: Mix all ingredients in a high-speed blender. You can process in an ice cream maker or store the mixture in a glass container and freeze.

Raspberry Sorbet: Mix all ingredients in a high-speed blender. You can process in an ice cream maker or store the mixture in a glass container and freeze.

Cherry-Vanilla: Mix bananas in a high-speed blender. Add dates and cherries, blend again, and then freeze. For toppings, try fresh coconut meat, frozen berries, pomegranate, strawberries, plantain chips, sweet pea shoots, cacao nibs, or whatever your heart desires.

Back to school
Falling leaves
Shorter days
Red. Purple. Gold. Orange
Harvest full of abundance
Persimmons. Apples. Plums
Thankful
Grateful
Rain. Sun. Rain
Umbrellas
Rain boots
Birds migrating
Animals hibernating
First snow

Autumn

Raw Detox

Yellow Sunshine Juice:
3 oranges
1/2 pineapple (without the skin)
1 apple
1 lemon
1 pear

Red Cranberry-Beet Juice:
2 cups fresh cranberries
4 beets
2 apples
1 lemon

Happy Carrot Juice:
6 carrots
1 orange
1 lime
1 apple
1/2 inch fresh ginger
1/2 inch fresh turmeric

Magic Berry Juice:
1 cup blackberries
3 small beets
1/2 cup cranberries
1 lemon
1 apple
1/4 small purple cabbage
1/2 inch fresh ginger

Happy Smoothie:
2 ripe bananas
1 pear
1 peach
1 apple
1 plum
1/2 cup blueberries

Fall is the perfect time to detox your body. Most of us live busy lives, eating unhealthy foods and spending long hours at the office. When you drink only juices, smoothies, and filtered water, you let your body heal. A mini detox (a day or two) will clean up your digestive system, energize you, and help destress your body and mind. During the cleanse, try to take time off from work, enjoy nature, take naps, and practice yoga.

Raw Cashew Milk:
1 cup raw cashews
3 cups filtered water
2 Medjool dates or 1–2 teaspoons raw coconut nectar or maple syrup
Pinch of pink Himalayan crystal salt or Celtic sea salt
1 teaspoon vanilla extract
1 ripe, frozen banana

Raw Cashew Milk: Mix all ingredients in a high-speed blender. Use nut milk bag. Garnish with cinnamon or turmeric powder. You can use other nuts in place of cashews, like macadamia, Brazil, hazelnuts, or almonds. Soak your nuts for 2–4 hours to help with digestion.

Stomach Soother Smoothie:
1 mango
3 grapefruits
1/2 lemon (with peel)
3 carrots
1/2 inch fresh ginger
2 cups baby spinach
Pinch of Ceylon cinnamon
Ripe banana (optional)

Stomach Soother Smoothie: Blend all ingredients in a high-speed blender. If made without banana, the Stomach Soother Smoothie will have a more bitter and gingery taste—great for stomach virus, morning sickness, flu, upset stomach, and overall energy. If made with banana, this smoothie will be sweeter and smoother.

Pumpkin-Cranberry Spaghetti

Serves 4

This simple dish tastes like fall pumpkin pie noodles.

Ingredients:
4 medium zucchini

Sauce:
5 ripe persimmons
1 large apple
3 tablespoons raw cranberries
1/3 cup fresh-squeezed orange juice
1 tablespoon fresh-squeezed lemon juice
1/2 small sugar pumpkin, cubed and without skin

Pasta: Run zucchini through a spiral pasta maker (e.g., Spirooli).

Instructions: Mix all ingredients in a high-speed blender or food processor. Pour sauce over noodles and sprinkle some pumpkin seeds and raw cranberries on top. You can even use part of the pumpkin as a serving dish. Just cut the pumpkin in half and scoop out the insides.

Falafel Salad

Serves 15

Raw Falafel:
1 cup walnuts
1 cup carrots, chopped
1 cup sun-dried tomatoes (soaked in filtered water for 30 minutes)
1 tablespoon chia seeds (soaked in 3 tablespoons water)
4 cloves garlic
1 teaspoon white sesame seeds
1/2 teaspoon curry powder
Pinch of cayenne pepper
1/3 teaspoon pink Himalayan crystal salt
1 teaspoon fresh thyme, chopped

Tahini Dressing:
3 tablespoons raw white tahini
3 tablespoons filtered water
1 tablespoon raw coconut vinegar or 1/2 lemon, juiced
Pinch of pink Himalayan crystal salt
Pinch of cayenne pepper

Falafel is a great addition to any salad. Also, try them with my Pasta Italiana (see recipe on page 57).

Instructions: Soak the sun-dried tomatoes. After 30 minutes, place all ingredients except for the sesame seeds in a food processor and process, but don't overprocess (similar to veggie burger recipe on page 79). Add sesame seeds and mix with a spoon. Next, using an ice cream scoop, make small falafel balls. They taste great just like this, but I like to dehydrate them for about 3–4 hours at 105°F to make them crunchy on the outside. You can also bake them in the oven on very low heat for 20 minutes if you don't have a dehydrator.

Tahini Dressing: Process all ingredients in a high-speed blender until smooth. Pour over your salad creation and enjoy.

For this salad, I used dino kale, red lettuce, baby tomatoes, small red peppers, carrots, cucumber, endive, red cabbage, and fresh herbs.

Fennel Salad with Orange & Pear

Serves 1-2

Ingredients:
1 fennel bulb
1 pear
1 orange
1/2 cup pomegranate seeds
10 raw cranberries
1/2 lemon, juiced
1/2 teaspoon hemp seed oil
Black pepper, to taste

Fall is so beautiful—a time to celebrate the abundance of Mother Nature's harvest. This salad makes a great light meal or appetizer.

Instructions: Slice fennel bulb, pear, and orange, and arrange on a plate. Top with pomegranate seeds, lemon juice, hemp seed oil, and black pepper. Add edible flowers for extra color, if desired.

Superfood Smoothie Bowl

Serves 2

Yellow Ingredients:
3 ripe bananas
3 ripe persimmons
1 small apple
2 Medjool dates
1/2 cup raw coconut water or filtered water
1/4 cup raw coconut meat, coconut cream,
or shredded coconut

Green Ingredients:
1 tablespoon spirulina powder
2 cups baby spinach
2 ripe bananas

When you're making a smoothie bowl, as opposed to a regular smoothie, be sure to make it very thick and creamy. Smoothies are actually meant to be chewed—not easily swallowed like juice. You can add frozen bananas to make it thicker and give it a consistency that resembles ice cream. Smoothies are very filling and should be eaten with a spoon, especially when you add nature's superfoods like berries, powders, nuts, or seeds. If you want to add extra crunch, try dried mulberries, buckwheat groats, or my gingerbread cookies made into granola crunch. Just follow the recipe on page 166, crumble the cookies, and sprinkle into a bowl.

Ingredients: Mix each color separately in a high-speed blender. Layer into a bowl and top with your favorite superfoods, like pumpkin seeds, chia seeds, raw cacao nibs, raspberries, blueberries, cranberries, shredded coconut, pomegranate seeds, and apple slices. Serve with fresh mint.

Chia Pudding with Almond Milk

Serves 2

Almond Milk:
1 cup raw almonds (soaked overnight)
3 cups filtered water
4 Medjool dates
Pinch of Ceylon cinnamon
Pinch of ginger powder
Pinch of cardamom
1 tablespoon maple syrup

Chia Pudding:
3 tablespoons chia seeds
1 cup filtered water

This is a very easy and quick meal for a healthy and yummy breakfast. To make chia pudding, you will need to make the almond milk first.

Almond Milk: After almonds have soaked overnight, mix all ingredients in a high-speed blender. You can strain the milk in a milk bag and use the pulp for cookies, or use the milk with the pulp in your chia pudding; it will be thick but so yummy—I prefer it with the pulp.

Instructions: In a large bowl, mix chia seeds with water and let sit for about 10–20 minutes. Mix well, and then add your raw almond milk (with or without the pulp). You can also add some oats and raw buckwheat sprouts for a different texture. Serve the chia pudding with sliced bananas, persimmons, and/or dried cranberries. Sprinkle cinnamon on top.

Pumpkin-Coconut Parfait

Serves 2-4

Ingredients:
1 1/2 cups raw sugar pumpkin, cubed
2-3 very ripe Hachiya persimmons
1 cup raw Jamaican coconut meat,
Thai young coconut meat,
or raw coconut butter
5-6 Medjool dates
Pinch of Ceylon cinnamon
Pinch of vanilla powder
2 tablespoons filtered water
3 tablespoons coconut water
Raw cranberries, for garnish

When I think of fall, I think of pumpkins and persimmons—they are a match made in heaven! This parfait isn't just beautiful to look at—it's absolutely delicious! It's sweet, pudding-like, and yummy.

Instructions: Scoop the meat from the coconut, and then in a high-speed blender or food processor mix raw coconut meat with 1 tablespoon coconut water or filtered water. Transfer to a dish, and then layer the white mixture at the bottom of your serving glass (keep half for next layer). Cut the sugar pumpkin in half, scoop out the seeds, peel off the skin, and cube. Next, in a high-speed blender mix pumpkin, persimmons, dates, vanilla, cinnamon, and 2 tablespoons coconut water or filtered water. Layer orange mixture on top of the white mixture (keep half for next layer), and then repeat the white and finish with the orange. Top with fresh cranberries. Tastes amazing with my Love Potion Truffles (see recipe on page 197).

Fall Juices

Serves 2

Cinnamon Sweet Potato Pie Juice:
1 small beet
2 uncooked sweet potatoes or yams
5 carrots
2 apples
2 oranges
1 lemon with peel (if not organic, use without peel)
1/2 inch ginger
Pinch of Ceylon cinnamon, for garnish

Fennel and Beet Magic Juice:
3 red beets
3 -4 kale leaves
1 cup spinach
1 lemon with peel (if not organic, use without peel)
5 carrots
1 pear
1 fennel bulb
1 cup red grapes

My favorite time of year is autumn; the leaves change color, and it's like pure magic. It's as if Mother Nature was saving this glorious beauty as a grand finale. The whole world looks like a colorful painting. Because the harvest happens in fall when everything is in season and tastes delicious, it's a great time to detox and cleanse the body. These are my favorite juice combos. The first juice tastes like a pumpkin pie milkshake and the second tastes like a delicious red wine.

Cinnamon Sweet Potato Pie Juice: Process all ingredients in a juicer. Shake together and serve. Garnish with cinnamon.

Fennel and Beet Magic Juice: Process all ingredients in a juicer. Shake together and serve.

Mizuna-Seaweed Salad

Serves 1-2

Enjoy this healthy salad as a lunch or appetizer.

Ingredients:

1 cup Mizuna greens, chopped
1 cup dried seaweed (soaked in filtered water for about 30 minutes)
1 cup baby tomatoes
1 teaspoon hemp seeds
1 teaspoon raw apple cider vinegar
Pinch of Celtic sea salt
1 teaspoon fresh-squeezed lemon juice
1 tablespoon red onion, chopped
1 cup purple cabbage, chopped

Instructions: Arrange ingredients as desired and garnish with sliced lemon and edible flowers. You can use a purple cabbage leaf as a serving dish. Sprinkle some freshly ground black pepper on top. Try pear or apple with walnuts for additional fall flavors and textures. If you don't have Mizuna greens, you can use other greens like baby lettuce, spinach, arugula, or mustard greens.

Buckwheat-Beet Pizza

Serves 2–4

Crust:

1 cup raw buckwheat (sprouted in filtered water overnight)
1 onion
1 beet
1 clove garlic
1/2 teaspoon Celtic sea salt
Pinch of cayenne pepper
3 tablespoons coconut flour
1 teaspoon raw coconut oil, melted
1/2 teaspoon curry powder

Tomato Sauce:

1/2 cup sun-dried tomatoes (soaked in filtered water for 30 minutes)
1/4 cup water from the tomatoes
2 cloves garlic
Celtic sea salt, to taste
Pinch of cayenne pepper
Pinch of cumin
1/2 lemon, juiced
5–7 leaves of fresh basil
1 cup baby tomatoes or cubed tomatoes

This beet pizza is not only beautiful to look at; it's super healthy, too! It's a great meal the whole family will enjoy.

Crust: Rinse and drain the sprouted buckwheat, and then process all ingredients in a food processor. Make little pizzas and place them on a Teflon sheet. Dehydrate at 110°F for about 5–8 hours, depending on how soft or dry you like your pizza crust. Flip over halfway.

Tomato Sauce: Mix all ingredients in a high-speed blender.

Presentation: When crust is ready, spread the sauce on the pizzas. Add sliced avocado, plantain chips (I make them while making the crust: slice very ripe plantains and dehydrate until crispy, about 8 hours), dried raw olives, shredded red cabbage, tomatoes, and fresh basil. You can also add raw macadamia cheese (see recipe on page 140). To warm, place pizzas in the dehydrator.

Cashew-Banana Brownies

Serves about 18

Ingredients:
4 large, ripe bananas
3 cups cashew meal
2 cups cacao powder
4 tablespoons maple syrup (or more if you prefer a sweeter dessert)
1 teaspoon Ceylon cinnamon
1 cup lucuma powder
1 teaspoon pink Himalayan crystal salt
2 cups filtered water

Additional ingredients if you want extra texture and sweetener:
1/2 cup walnuts
1/2 cup dried, unsulphured cherries or mulberries

Who doesn't love chocolate brownies? These brownies are so delicious and good for you that you can enjoy them anytime—even for breakfast.

Instructions: In a large bowl, mix all ingredients except the bananas and water. In a separate bowl, smash bananas with a fork, and then add them to the dry ingredients. Slowly, add the water and mix until smooth. Add walnuts and cherries or mulberries, if desired. Line a glass pan with parchment paper and pour the mixture on top. Using a spoon, spread the mixture evenly in the pan. Place the brownies at the bottom of the dehydrator at 110°F for about 6 hours. At this point, they will be warm, soft, and gooey, and you can eat them like this or take them out of the glass pan with the parchment paper and dehydrate for another 6-8 hours or until they are firm. If you don't have a dehydrator, you can bake them on the lowest setting of your oven for about 20-30 minutes. They won't be 100% raw, but they will still be yummy and good for you!

To speed up the process, cut brownies into small pieces. They are ready when they are chewy inside and crunchy outside. You can eat them plain or add a thin layer of raw chocolate on top. To make raw chocolate, see recipe on page 53. Pour thin layer of raw chocolate on top of the brownies and place in the fridge to set. Serve them with fresh fruits like raspberries, figs, and pomegranates. Keep brownies in the fridge for up to a few days or freeze for later.

Persimmon Salad

Serves 2–4

Salad:
1 cup red grapes
3 ripe persimmons, cubed
1/2 red onion, chopped
1 ripe banana, cubed
1 cup purple cabbage, shredded
1 small apple, cubed

Dressing:
1 orange, juiced
1/2 lemon, juiced
1 teaspoon raw apple cider vinegar
1/2 teaspoon Celtic sea salt
Pinch of cayenne pepper
1 teaspoon curry powder
1 teaspoon hemp seeds

This fruity salad with curry flavor is perfect as a side dish and can be paired with so many different main courses. Try it with raw pasta or lasagna!

Salad: Arrange all salad ingredients as desired. Sprinkle hemp seeds on top.

Dressing: Process all dressing ingredients in a high-speed blender until smooth. Pour over salad and enjoy.

Raw Cheese Plate

Serves 6

Almond Cheese:
2 1/2 cups raw almonds
(soaked in filtered water for 8 hours, then drained)

Almond Brie:
1 1/2 cups almond pulp
1/2 teaspoon Celtic sea salt
1 teaspoon vegan probiotic
Pinch of cayenne pepper
1 teaspoon nutritional yeast
Raw garlic, fresh herbs, onion flakes, or lemon juice, to taste (optional)

Crunchy Almond Cheese:
2 cups almond pulp
1/2 teaspoon Celtic sea salt
1 teaspoon vegan probiotic
Pinch of cayenne pepper
1 teaspoon nutritional yeast
1/2 teaspoon curry powder
Pinch of fresh black pepper
1/2 teaspoon dried tarragon leaves

Macadamia Nut Ricotta:
2 cups raw macadamia nuts

Macadamia Cheese:
1 1/2 cup Macadamia nut pulp
1/3 teaspoon Celtic sea salt
1 teaspoon vegan probiotic
1 teaspoon dried onion flakes
1/3 teaspoon nutritional yeast
Dried rosemary, thyme (optional)

Nut cheeses are a perfect substitute for dairy cheese and are great additions to salads, soups, pizza, and raw appetizers.

Almond Cheese: Place almonds in a high-speed blender. Cover the almonds with filtered water and mix well. Using a nut milk bag, strain the mixture. The almond pulp will be used to make a cheese, and the remainder is almond milk, to which you can add some dates, maple syrup, cinnamon, and a pinch of Himalayan pink crystal salt. Almond milk is great in smoothies, desserts, chia pudding, and more.

Almond Brie: Mix all ingredients until well combined. To make hard cheese, form mixture into your desired shape, and then place in the dehydrator at 115°F for about 8–12 hours or more, depending on how soft you like your cheese.

Crunchy Almond Cheese: Mix all ingredients until well combined, and then spread mixture onto a Teflon sheet and dehydrate at 115°F until dry. Flip it over halfway. Break into pieces and store in a glass container in the fridge for up to 2-3 weeks.

Macadamia Nut Ricotta: Place macadamia nuts in a high-speed blender. Cover the nuts with filtered water and mix well. Using a nut milk bag, strain the mixture. Use the strained milk for desserts or smoothies. Use the pulp as a vegan ricotta cheese—perfect on my Pasta Italiana (see recipe on page 57).

Macadamia Cheese: Mix all ingredients until well combined, and then form a shape—I chose a circle—and place it on a Teflon sheet. Dehydrate at 115°F for 12 hours (flip it over halfway). Keep in the fridge for up to 3-5 days. For the look of blue cheese, add a pinch of spirulina powder to the mixture.

Banana Crepes

Serves 4–6

Crepes:
5-6 ripe bananas
Pinch of Ceylon cinnamon
1/2 lemon, juiced

Filling:
2 cups cashews (soaked
in filtered water for 2 hours)
1 cup water, coconut water, or coconut milk
2-3 tablespoons maple syrup
or a few Medjool dates
1/3 teaspoon medicinal vanilla
or vanilla extract

Back in Poland, I used to love crepes, called *Nalesniki*, but they were made with white flour and cheese, and they were fried. I created this dish so I could enjoy a healthier version of my favorite dessert. These crepes are light, delicious, and so easy to make. Try adding essential oils or vanilla extract for different flavors, fruits like blueberries or raspberries, or raw cacao powder or carob powder—there is so much you can do. This recipe is also delicious with shredded coconut, dried mulberries, and/or berry or passion fruit sauce.

Crepes: Mix all ingredients in a high-speed blender until smooth. You can add raw sweet potatoes or butternut squash, mango, pear, apple, or berries, if desired—I used only bananas. Next, transfer mixture onto a Teflon sheet, creating pancake shapes, and dehydrate at 110°F for about 4–5 hours, or longer.

Filling: Soak cashews. When they are ready, mix all ingredients in a high-speed blender until smooth. For a low-fat option, use frozen bananas with dates for the filling; it will taste just like ice cream. Serve with fresh fruits and mint (my favorites are raspberries and pomegranates).

Polish Stuffed Cabbage

Serves 2

Wraps:
2 large, soft cabbage leaves (from inside not outside so you can wrap them easily)

Stuffing:
2 cups baby arugula
1 cup sun-dried tomatoes
(soaked in filtered water for 1 hour)
4-5 tablespoons sunflower seeds
(soaked in filtered water for 1 hour)
1 cup Hinoki mushrooms
1 orange, cubed
1 small onion
1/2 cup fresh pomegranate seeds
1 ripe persimmon
Pink Himalayan crystal salt, to taste Fresh black pepper, to taste
1/2 lemon, juiced
1 tablespoon hemp seed oil or chia seed oil

Stuffed cabbage is one of the most famous dishes in Poland. While experimenting with different flavors, I came up with this raw, plant-based version of a classic Polish dish.

Instructions: Start by soaking sun-dried tomatoes and sunflower seeds. Drain the water, and then mix in a high-speed blender. When ready, chop all stuffing ingredients except arugula, and mix everything in a large bowl. Use cabbage leaves as wraps. Serve immediately with greens on the side.

Piña Colada Cake

Serves 10

Crust:
2 cups shredded coconut
8 Medjool dates
1/3 teaspoon pink Himalayan crystal salt
Pinch of cayenne pepper
4 tablespoons yacón syrup or maple syrup
1 cup raw cacao powder
1 tablespoon vanilla powder
1/2 cup coconut oil, melted
1 tablespoon orange blossom water
1 cup dried mulberries
2 tablespoons mesquite powder
or lucuma powder

Filling:
2 1/2 cups raw cashews
(soaked in filtered water for 1 hour)
1/2 cup flesh from Thai young coconut
(or use raw coconut butter)
3 cups fresh pineapple, cubed
1 ripe mango, peeled
8 Medjool dates
1 ripe banana
1 tablespoon maple syrup (or more
if you prefer a sweeter dessert)
1/2 teaspoon vanilla extract

Chocolate Topping:
2 tablespoons coconut oil
2 tablespoons raw cacao powder
1 tablespoon maple syrup
1/2 teaspoon vanilla extract

This cake crust recipe works for truffle brownies as well. Simply make little truffle balls and place in the fridge to set.

Crust: Process all ingredients in a food processor; you may need to stop periodically to scrape the sides. When finished, place the mixture in the bottom of a large cake dish, and, using a spoon, press down evenly.

Filling: Process all ingredients in a food processor until smooth, and then pour mixture over crust and spread evenly with a spatula. Freeze for a few hours or overnight, until set. If you love chocolate, you can make a raw chocolate topping, but it tastes great without it, too.

Chocolate Topping: Process all ingredients in a food processor until smooth, and then drizzle over cake. Keep the cake in the freezer until ready to eat. Decorate with fresh fruits, herbs, shredded coconut, and/or edible flowers. You can even add some raw chocolates (see recipe on page 199).

Raw Almond Butter Cups

Serves 12

Raw Chocolate:
1 cup raw cacao butter
5 tablespoons coconut oil
1 1/2 cups raw cacao powder
Pinch of pink Himalayan crystal salt
1 tablespoon lucuma powder
Pinch of cayenne pepper
5 tablespoons maple syrup (or more if you prefer sweeter chocolate)
1/2 teaspoon medicinal vanilla or vanilla extract or powder

Filling:
Raw almond butter

These almond butter cups are perfect as a healthy snack or dessert.

Instructions: Melt cacao butter and coconut oil on very low heat, about 105-110°F. Use a double boiler so you can temper the chocolate. Add cacao powder and mix slowly with a wooden spoon. Next, add the rest of the ingredients and keep mixing until perfectly smooth. Fill chocolate molds or paper or silicone cups halfway with chocolate mixture, and then add a scoop of raw almond butter. Finish the cups with another layer of chocolate. Place in the fridge to set. You can sprinkle some salt on the top. Store in a glass container in the fridge or freeze for up to 8 weeks.

Additional Option: Experiment with different flavors by adding dried fruits, nuts, or essential oils to your chocolate almond butter cups. My favorite essential oil flavors are orange and peppermint, and I love making this recipe with dried prunes. You can also use coconut butter, cashew butter, hazelnut butter, or peanut butter.

Polish Leek–Apple Salad

Serves 2-4

Ingredients:
2 leeks
3 sweet apples
3 carrots
1 tablespoon fresh lemon juice
1 tablespoon raw apple cider vinegar
1 tablespoon flaxseed oil or chia seed oil
Ceylon cinnamon, to taste
Pink Himalayan crystal salt, to taste
Fresh black pepper, to taste

This salad is very popular in Poland during the fall/winter season, and this is my own vegan version of it. It is flavorful, very healthy, and easy to make.

Instructions: Wash the leeks very carefully, and then slice them with a sharp knife. Place leeks in a glass bowl, add salt and lemon juice, and let marinate for 10–20 minutes. Next, shred the carrots and apples, add them to the leeks along with the rest of the ingredients, and arrange as desired. You can also add pears, raisins, or persimmons.

Moroccan Cabbage Salad

Serves 2

Ingredients:
2 cups white cabbage, chopped
1/3 cup hazelnuts
1 prickly pear, sliced
Few pieces of fresh mint
1/3 teaspoon curry powder
Pinch of cumin
1 tablespoon apple cider vinegar
Celtic sea salt, to taste

When I visited Morocco, I was so inspired by all the incredible, fresh, exotic spices and flavors. I wanted to create something inspired by my trip, so I came up with this dish. This is a great salad for an appetizer or lunch.

Instructions: Mix cabbage, hazelnuts, curry powder, cumin, and salt, and follow with apple cider vinegar. Toss and serve. Serve the sliced prickly pear as desired on the side. Garnish with fresh mint, edible flowers, and dates.

Dark nights
White snow
Go within
Dreaming
Find your miracle
Forgive, let go, be free
Sitting by the fire
Warm pj's and socks
Snow days
Holidays and family gatherings
Hope, love, and joy
So much love
It is so freezing cold

Winter

Salads on the Go

Salad:
2 oranges, sliced
3 cups baby spinach
3 cups baby arugula
1 cup fresh raspberries
1/2 cup pineapple, cubed
1 cup blueberries
2 cups strawberries, sliced
4 radishes, sliced
1 cup broccoli, cut into small pieces
4-5 tablespoons hazelnuts
4-5 tablespoons almonds
2 tablespoons red onion, chopped

Dressing:
1 tablespoon raw apple cider vinegar
1/2 lemon, juiced
1/2 cup pineapple, cubed
1/2 teaspoon nutritional yeast
1/2 teaspoon filtered water
1 teaspoon chia seed oil

Take this great rainbow salad with you to work, for a hike, in your car—wherever you're going. You can prepare multiple salads the night before and just keep the dressing on the side. Easy, fast, and nutritious. You will need 4 large mason jars.

Salad: Layer all salad ingredients into 4 mason jars.

Dressing: Mix all ingredients in a high-speed blender. Drizzle over salad and enjoy immediately or serve on the side.

Olenko's Winterland Parfait

Serves 2–4

White (Cool):
1 cup cashews (soaked
in filtered water for 1 hour)
1 ripe banana
1/2 teaspoon vanilla extract
1-2 tablespoons maple syrup
or coconut nectar
5 tablespoons fresh coconut water, coconut
milk, or filtered water
5 tablespoons fresh coconut meat
or shredded coconut
1 tablespoon coconut butter
2–3 drops of therapeutic-grade
peppermint essential oil

Orange (Warm):
5 ripe persimmons
2 ripe, frozen bananas
1 tablespoon mesquite powder
or lucuma powder
5-6 Medjool dates
Pinch of Ceylon cinnamon
1/2 teaspoon molasses
2 tablespoons fresh coconut water

Toppings:
Raw cacao beans
Fresh thyme
Goji berries
Persimmon

This is my favorite dessert creation, and it's perfect for the holiday season! Enjoy both warm and cool sensations with each layer—it's so delicious! Make sure the persimmons are very ripe, as it will create a smooth, sweet, pumpkin-like flavor and velvety texture.
If you want to add extra crunch, try adding my gingerbread cookies made into granola crunch. Just follow the recipe on page 166, crumble the cookies, and sprinkle on the top.

Instructions: Mix white portion in a high-speed blender. Use half the mixture to layer into the bottom of your serving glass(es) and transfer the rest into a small bowl. Rinse the blender, and then mix the orange portion. Pour the orange mixture over the white layer, and then finish with the rest of the white mixture. Decorate this dessert with raw cacao nibs, goji berries, greens, and fresh-cut persimmons.

Additional Options: If you don't have fresh coconut water, use filtered water instead. If you don't have lucuma or mesquite powders, just use more dates.

Beetroot Wrap

Makes 2 large wraps

Wraps:
3 medium beetroots, peeled and cubed
(about 2 cups)
1 celery stick, chopped
1 small onion, chopped
1/3 teaspoon Celtic sea salt
Pinch of fresh black pepper
1 teaspoon flax seeds and 1 teaspoon
chia seeds (soaked in 2 tablespoons
water for 10 minutes)
1 clove garlic
5 tablespoons filtered water
1 ripe banana
1 teaspoon nutritional yeast,
for garnish

Filling:
Radishes
Baby arugula
Peppers
Sweet pea shoots
Tomatoes
Cucumbers
Pomegranate seeds
Raw tahini
Lemon juice
Fresh basil
Celtic sea salt
Cayenne pepper

These raw beet wraps are a healthy substitute for flour tortillas.

Wraps: Start by soaking the seeds. Then, when ready, blend all ingredients in a high-speed blender until creamy. Spread the mixture into a 1/8-inch-thick layer on Teflon sheets. You can sprinkle some nutritional yeast on top for a cheesy flavor or flavor with fresh herbs, if desired. Dehydrate for 1 hour at 115°F, and then lower the temperature to 110°F for about 2–3 hours. Dehydrate until your wraps are dry but still flexible. It should take about 4–5 hours total, depending on the size and thickness of your wraps. When ready, peel the wraps off the Teflon sheets and cut them with kitchen scissors into desired shapes. Store for up to 7 days at room temperature in a glass container.

For the Filling: Spread some raw tahini on your wrap and sprinkle spices on top. Chop all the veggies, place inside wrap, and fold over. Garnish with sliced lemons, oranges, greens, and edible flowers. Serve with plantain chips (recipe on page 135).

Winter Snowballs

Serves 25-30

Ingredients:
2 cups raw almonds
12-14 Medjool dates
4 tablespoons raw cacao powder
1 cup raw pumpkin seeds
2 tablespoons ginger powder
2 tablespoons pumpkin spice
2 tablespoons lucuma powder
3 tablespoons filtered water
(or a bit more)

Toppings:
Goji berries
Raw pistachios
Shredded coconut
Raw cacao powder
Lucuma powder

These yummy snowballs make a great healthy snack, holiday dessert, or homemade Christmas present. You can make them with friends, family, or kids as a snack for Santa. They remind me of my childhood and playing for long hours in the snow with my friends.

Instructions: Combine all ingredients in a food processor and pulse. You'll want to see small pieces of the almonds in the paste. Stop pulsing when all ingredients start to stick together. Clean your hands and, using a spoon, scoop the paste from the food processor and form balls with your hands. Place desired toppings in small bowls, and then roll each ball in your topping of choice. It's a little messy but really fun. Store snowballs in a glass container in the fridge for up to 5 days or freeze and enjoy later.

Gingerbread House & Cookies

Serves 20

Ingredients:

3 cups almond meal (or whole, raw almonds that you grind in a food processor)
1 cup coconut flour
1 cup shredded coconut flakes
2 teaspoons Ceylon cinnamon
4 tablespoons ground ginger powder (I like my cookies very gingery; you can use less, if desired)
1 teaspoon pumpkin pie spice (a blend of cinnamon, ginger, cloves, lemon peel, and cardamom)
2-3 tablespoons Blackstrap unsulphured molasses
5 tablespoons maple syrup

When I think of winter, I think of the Christmas holiday, and when I think of Christmas, I think of a gingerbread house and cookies.

Instructions: Mix all ingredients together in a large bowl using your hands (or use a food processor). The dough should be soft and sticky, so add more maple syrup or filtered water if needed. Using a rolling pin, roll the dough over a large cutting board (place parchment paper between so the dough won't stick). Form the dough into gingerbread man shapes, stars, or Christmas trees (you can use cookie cutters for this). Use geometric shapes of your choosing to make a gingerbread house. I cut geometric shapes from paper and used them as a stencil. The number of cookies will depend on the size of your cookies.

The batter will be a little sticky but very workable. If too soft, refrigerate for 30 minutes or place in the freezer for 5 minutes. Flatten the dough using your hands, form little pancakes, and sprinkle with shredded coconut. You can:

- Eat the cookies like this, soft.
- Dehydrate at 110°F for 5-8 hours. Store cookies in a glass container in the fridge for up to a week or freeze for later.
- Use a dehydrator to warm up your cookies. Serve with fresh, homemade almond milk, tea, or a smoothie.
- Bake cookies on a very low setting in the oven (e.g., 300°F for 8-12 minutes).
- Decorate them with raw chocolate (follow instructions on page 53). Pour raw chocolate over the prepared cookies and sprinkle almonds or goji berries and shredded coconut flakes on top. When you serve your gingerbread cookies, decorate them with dried and fresh fruits.

Gingerbread Man Smoothie

Serves 1–2

Ingredients:
1/2 cup Brazil nuts
2 cups baby spinach
4 ripe bananas
3 ripe persimmons
1 pear
3-4 dates
Pinch of Ceylon cinnamon
1 1/2 cups filtered water

It can be challenging to stay on track with a healthy diet during the holidays. A green smoothie is a fast, easy, and healthy choice for breakfast or as an afternoon snack. This one tastes like dessert but is extremely healthy, so no guilt! Enjoy, and Happy Holidays!

Instructions: Process all ingredients in a high-speed blender. Top with fresh pomegranate seeds and serve with gingerbread man cookies (see recipe on page 166).

Berry-Date Chocolate Bars

Serves about 20

Base:
1/2 cup raw buckwheat groats
2 1/2 cups Medjool dates, pitted
1 cup dried, unsulphured
mulberries
1/2 cup dried, unsulphured
aronia berries
1/2 cup dried, unsulphured cherries
3-4 tablespoons pumpkin seeds
1/3 cup raw, gluten-free oats

Raw Chocolate:
1 cup raw cacao powder
5 tablespoons coconut oil
1/2 cup cacao butter
3-4 tablespoons coconut nectar
or maple syrup
2 tablespoons lucuma powder
1/4 teaspoon reishi powder
or chaga mushroom powder (optional)
1/2 teaspoon medicinal vanilla
or vanilla extract
1/5 teaspoon pink Himalayan crystal salt
Pinch of cayenne pepper

I've prepared this recipe with many different kinds of dried fruits (prunes, apricots, pineapple, and figs) and all kinds of nuts and seeds, and each iteration is equally delicious. Have fun with it and create your own favorite mix!

Base: Line a large glass pan with parchment paper and spread buckwheat groats evenly in the bottom of the pan. Next, using a food processor, process the dates, and then spread them on top of the buckwheat groats. Sprinkle all the dried fruits next. You can add some spices like cinnamon or cardamom, if desired.

Raw Chocolate: Melt cacao butter and coconut oil on very low heat, about 105–110°F. Use a double boiler so you can temper the chocolate. Add cacao powder and mix slowly with a wooden spoon. Next, add the rest of the ingredients and keep mixing until perfectly smooth. Pour raw chocolate over base and sprinkle oats on top. Let set in the fridge for about 1 hour. Take out and cut into desired shapes. Store in a glass container in the fridge for up to a few weeks or freeze. Serve with fresh raspberries and pomegranate seeds for a fancy, healthy dessert that's perfect to enjoy at home or to bring to a holiday gathering.

Carrot-Beet Mandala Salad

Serves 2–4

Salad Mandala:
3 oranges, sliced
4 red beets, shredded
6 carrots, shredded
1 apple, shredded
2 cups baby spinach
Bunch of purple curly kale
1 cup baby tomatoes
1 starfruit

Dressing:
1 cup cashews or macadamia nuts
3 tablespoons apple cider vinegar
Pinch of pink Himalayan crystal salt
Pinch of fresh black pepper
1 lemon, juiced
Pinch of nutritional yeast (for cheesy taste)
1 cup filtered water
1 clove garlic (optional)

Carrots and beets are root vegetables, which contain lots of important vitamins and nutrients. Enjoy this salad as a side dish or main course.

Salad Mandala: Arrange kale leaves, oranges, and spinach in a big bowl (use two oranges and keep one for the flower). Then, starting from the middle, place shredded beets, then apples, and then cover the apples with shredded carrots (apples turn brown very quickly after you shred them, so keep this in mind when serving this dish). Next, peel an orange and make into a flower. Decorate with sliced starfruit and baby tomatoes. You can also chop the kale leaves and mix everything for a more casual salad.

Dressing: Mix all ingredients in a high-speed blender. Serve on the side or pour over your salad.

Persimmon-Pumpkin Cake

Serves 10–12

Base:
2 cups Medjool dates
1 cup walnuts
1 cup dried, unsulphured
mulberries
1/4 teaspoon Ceylon cinnamon
1/4 teaspoon ginger powder
1 teaspoon fresh lime juice

Filling:
1 1/2 cups sugar pumpkin, cubed
4–5 ripe persimmons
1 ripe banana
1 cup cashews or macadamia nuts
(soaked in filtered water for 30 minutes)
2 tablespoons fresh meat from Thai young
coconuts or shredded coconut
1 tablespoon coconut butter
1 tablespoon lucuma powder
1 teaspoon maple syrup
2 tablespoons fresh-squeezed lemon juice
1/4 teaspoon Ceylon cinnamon

Persimmon, pumpkin, and pomegranate are the perfect combination for this festive holiday cake. Share this delicious treat with your family and friends.

Base: Sprinkle mulberries and walnuts on the bottom of a medium springform pan. Open your dates, take out the pits, and place the pitted dates on top of the mulberries and walnuts. Sprinkle spices and lime juice over the top. You can also process this in a food processor.

Filling: Mix all ingredients in a food processor or high-speed blender. If too thick, add a tablespoon or two of fresh coconut water or filtered water. Pour over the base and place in the freezer to set, about 5 hours. Serve with fresh herbs, pomegranate seeds, and raw figs.

Magical Parfait

Serves 3-4

Chia-Cacao Layer:
2 tablespoons chia seeds
(soaked in 4 tablespoons filtered water for
10 minutes)
2/3 cup Brazil nuts
Pinch of cardamom
Pinch of Ceylon cinnamon
Pinch of Celtic sea salt
1/2 cup filtered water
3 tablespoons carob powder
1 tablespoon raw cacao powder
1 teaspoon maple syrup

Banana-Cherry Layer:
2 cups frozen cherries, pitted
4 -5 ripe, frozen bananas
1/2 cup filtered water

This is a great healthy dessert. Simple, beautiful, and easy to make.

Chia-Cacao Layer: Mix all ingredients in a high-speed blender. Set aside and rinse blender.

Banana-Cherry Layer: Mix all ingredients in a high-speed blender.

Instructions: Layer both mixtures in your glass(es) and serve immediately. You can add another layer with plain soaked chia seeds, if desired. Top it off with shredded coconut, frozen cherries, and fresh herbs.

Peasant Celeriac Salad

Serves 2-4

Salad:
2 large celeriac roots (without the skin), shredded
2 sweet, juicy apples, shredded
1 small red onion, chopped
1/2 cup walnuts
1/2 cup dried, unsulphured cranberries
1/4 cup raw cranberries
Fresh mint, for garnish

Dressing:
1 lemon, juiced
1/4 teaspoon Ceylon cinnamon
1 teaspoon fresh parsley, chopped
3 tablespoons raw apple cider vinegar
1 tablespoon flaxseed oil, hemp seed oil, or chia seed oil
Pinch of Celtic sea salt
Pinch of fresh black pepper
Pinch of cumin

Simple food is the best. During the cold winter months, it's good to eat local fruits like apples and pears, and root vegetables like beets, celeriac, and leeks. This recipe is inspired by a very popular Polish salad.

Salad: Cut the celeriac roots in half, shave off the thick skin, and rinse well. Shred roots and apples on a coarse grating board and chop the onion. Mix roots, apples, and onion in a large bowl.

Dressing: Mix all ingredients in a small bowl. Pour dressing over salad and let marinate for 20–30 minutes. Add nuts and fruits. Decorate with cranberries and fresh mint, and serve. For a more festive holiday dish, add fresh oranges, pears, grapes, or pomegranate seeds.

Frosty Banana Nice Cream

Serves 2

Ingredients:
10 ripe, frozen bananas
3–4 Medjool dates, pitted
1/4 cup coconut water, nondairy milk,
or filtered water
1/2 teaspoon vanilla extract

Banana ice cream (aka nana ice cream or nice cream) is my favorite meal. As I child, I used to love eating ice cream during cold Polish winters after returning home from school. One of my other favorite winter memories was making a snowman as a child. I created this recipe to celebrate my love for ice cream and snow. Transforming ripe, frozen bananas into yummy, low-fat, creamy, soft-serve ice cream is pure magic. Enjoy for breakfast; it's completely guilt-free. For a little variation, add frozen fruits like berries, mango, or pineapple, or raw cacao or carob powder for a chocolate flavor.

Instructions: To make ice cream, you will need ripe, frozen bananas. The more spotty your bananas, the better, as it will make your ice cream naturally sweet. Simply peel the bananas, break them into pieces, and freeze. Once frozen, blend bananas and all other ingredients in a high-speed blender or food processor; you may need to stop periodically to scrape the sides. Mix until smooth. For different flavors, add fruit to the vanilla ice cream and blend. For a chocolate flavor, mix base ingredients with 1 teaspoon raw carob powder or 1/2 teaspoon raw cacao powder. Top with nuts, seeds, shredded coconut, dried or fresh fruits, and/or raw chocolate.

Kale-Pomegranate Pasta

Serves 2–4

Pasta:
2 medium zucchini

Green Sauce:
2 avocados
1 lemon
Pinch of pink Himalayan crystal salt
1 cup arugula

Toppings:
Seeds from 1 pomegranate
Almonds
Cranberries
Sprinkle of nutritional yeast (optional)
Pinch of cayenne pepper

Kale is one of the healthiest plant foods. It has many medicinal properties and contains vitamins A, K, C, B6, B1, B2, and B3, as well as minerals like manganese, calcium, potassium, and magnesium.

Pasta: Run zucchini through a spiral pasta maker (e.g., Spirooli).

Presentation: Arrange kale leaves on a plate, and then arrange your raw zucchini noodles on top. In a high-speed blender, prepare green sauce. Pour over pasta. Top with pomegranate seeds, raw almonds, and cranberries. Sprinkle some nutritional yeast on top, if desired. Serve immediately.

Rainbow Salad

Serves 1

Salad:
1 cup baby tomatoes
1 cup radishes, sliced
2 carrots, cut lengthwise
1 cup cucumber, sliced
1 cup sweet peas
1 blood orange, sliced
1 cup purple cabbage, shredded
3 celery stalks, cut into 2-inch pieces
Few pieces of different-colored
baby lettuce and spinach
Few pieces of scallions

Dressing:
1 ripe avocado
1/2 lemon, juiced
Pinch of Celtic sea salt
Pinch of cayenne pepper
1 clove garlic, chopped
Fresh parsley

When it's cold, we often don't get enough fresh air and vitamin D. It's important to eat a variety of fruits and veggies to get
essential vitamins and minerals so we don't get sick. Eat the rainbow every day!

Salad: Chop all veggies and arrange on a plate.

Dressing: Mix all ingredients in a high-speed blender. Serve over salad or on the side.

Moroccan Carrot Salad

Serves 1-2

Salad:
5 medium carrots, shredded
Seeds from 1 pomegranate
1 raw fig
Cranberries, for garnish
Fresh mint, for garnish

Dressing:
2 oranges, juiced
1 teaspoon rose water
Pinch of Ceylon cinnamon
Pinch of cardamom powder
1 teaspoon raw coconut nectar
1/2 lemon, juiced

This salad is beautiful as an appetizer or a healthy lunch on a cold winter day.

Instructions: Mix all dressing ingredients in a high-speed blender and pour over shredded carrots. Marinate for 10 minutes. Transfer to a serving bowl and decorate with pomegranate seeds. Cut 1 fresh fig like a flower and decorate with fresh cranberries and fresh mint leaves. For a more complex salad, add pecans, pistachios, chopped dates, raisins, dried mulberries, and/or apricots.

Red Velvet Cake

Serves 10

Cake:
4 cups raw red beets, cubed
2 cups Medjool dates, pitted
3-4 tablespoons walnuts
1/3 teaspoon Ceylon cinnamon

Filling and Frosting:
2 ripe bananas
1 cup raw coconut water
2/3 cup dried figs
1 teaspoon rose water
1 1/2 cups cashews (soaked in filtered water for 1 hour)
1/2 cup shredded coconut or raw coconut butter

This recipe, which can be prepared as one cake or cupcakes, is perfect for birthdays, Valentine's Day, or a holiday party.

Cake: Mix all ingredients in a food processor. Press half of the mixture into the bottom of a medium-size springform pan or cupcake molds.

Filling and Frosting: Mix all ingredients in a high-speed blender and process until smooth. Layer half over the red base, and then follow with another layer of red. Use the rest of the filling/frosting mixture to frost the top of your cake or cupcakes. Sprinkle some shredded coconut on top, if desired. Place in the freezer until set, about 6 hours or overnight. When ready to serve, garnish with fresh lemon zest, pistachios, goji berries, strawberries, and/or cranberries.

Cosmic Rainbow Smoothie Bowl

Serves 6–8

Red:
2 cups frozen raspberries
1 cup fresh raspberries

Orange:
3 tablespoons fresh orange juice
or filtered water
6-7 ripe persimmons

Yellow:
1 mango
1/2 pineapple, cubed (about 2 cups)
2 ripe bananas
1 cup frozen peaches

Green:
4 cups baby spinach
1/4 pineapple, cubed (about 1 cup)

Blue:
2 ripe bananas
1 1/2 cups cashews
2 tablespoons fresh coconut water
Pinch of Blue Majik powder

Purple:
3 ripe bananas
2 Medjool dates
1 tablespoon acai powder
1 cup blueberries

Share this beautiful recipe with your family as a breakfast bowl or bring it with you to a holiday party.

Instructions: Mix each color separately in a high-speed blender, making sure to rinse the blender between each color. Gently layer in a very large glass bowl. Serve immediately.

Winter Cake

Serves 10

Crust:
5 tablespoons raw almonds
4 tablespoons dried mulberries
12–14 Medjool dates (about 2 cups)

Filling:
3 cups raw cashews (soaked
in filtered water for 3–4 hours)
2 tablespoons fresh lemon juice
4 tablespoons maple syrup
2-3 tablespoons lucuma powder
3 tablespoons coconut cream
2 large, ripe bananas
2-3 tablespoons dried mulberries
1 cup raw coconut water or coconut milk
1/8 teaspoon Blue Majik powder
1–2 drops of lime essential oil (optional)

This cake looks like it's from a magical winter kingdom. It's perfect for a special occasion or holiday party–so light and delicious!

Crust: Process all ingredients in a food processor, and then press to the bottom of a medium springform pan.

Filling: Mix all ingredients except Blue Majik powder in a high-speed blender or food processor. Pour 3/4 of the mixture over the crust. Add blue powder to remaining mixture and process. Layer it on top of the cake. Freeze cake for about 8 hours or overnight. Decorate when ready to serve. Make a snowflake shape with a cookie cutter using fresh jicama or apple and sprinkle some shredded coconut and Blue Majik powder on top for a pretty blue color. Serve with fresh blueberries and blackberries.

Love Potion Truffles

Serves 20

Truffles:
3 cups Medjool dates
1/4 teaspoon Ceylon cinnamon
1/2 cup walnuts, chopped or
smashed with fork
Almonds, hazelnuts, or shredded coconut
can be used insted of walnuts

Raw Chocolate:
1/2 cup raw cacao butter
1/2 cup raw coconut oil
2 cups cacao powder
Pinch of cayenne pepper
Pinch of pink Himalayan crystal salt
1 teaspoon chaga mushroom
powder (optional)
1-2 teaspoons lucuma powder (optional)
1 tablespoon reishi powder (optional)
3-4 tablespoons maple syrup

1 teaspoon medicinal vanilla
or vanilla extract

These truffles are a huge hit in my house, and they are so easy to make. Watch out, though—they have special love powers.

Truffles: Process dates in a food processor, and then add other ingredients. Form truffle balls using your hands.

Raw Chocolate: Melt cacao butter and coconut oil on very low heat, about 105–110°F. Use a double boiler so you can temper the chocolate. Add cacao powder and mix slowly with a wooden spoon. Next, add the rest of the ingredients and keep mixing until perfectly smooth. Coat truffles in raw chocolate, and then place them on a plate so the chocolate can set. You can place them in the freezer for 5–10 minutes, and then dip them again for an extra-thick chocolate coating. Store in a glass container in the fridge for up to a few weeks.

*Use leftover chocolate mix and make some raw chocolates. Follow recipie on page 199.

Valentine's Chocolates

Serves about 15

Chocolates:
1 cup raw cacao butter
5 tablespoons coconut oil
1 1/2 cups raw cacao powder
5 tablespoons maple syrup or date sugar
1/8 teaspoon Celtic sea salt
Pinch of cayenne pepper
1/2 teaspoon medicinal vanilla
or vanilla extract
1-2 tablespoons lucuma powder

Filling Options:
Raw coconut cream
Raw cashew butter
Apricots
Hazelnuts
Almonds
Dried mangos
Prunes
Mulberries
Dried cherries soaked in rum
*Few drops of therapeutic-grade essential
oils, like lavender, peppermint, orange,
rose, or frankincense*

These raw chocolates make the perfect Valentine's Day gift.

Instructions: Melt cacao butter and coconut oil on very low heat, about 105–110°F. Use a double boiler so you can temper the chocolate. Add cacao powder and mix slowly with a wooden spoon. Add the rest of the ingredients and keep mixing until perfectly smooth. Pour chocolate halfway into molds, saving about half the mixture for the next layer. Place desired fillings on top of bottom layer of chocolate, and then fill molds with the rest of the chocolate. Let set in the fridge. Serve over fresh rose petals. Store in a glass container in the fridge for up to 12 weeks.

CPSIA information can be obtained at www.ICGtesting.com
Printed in the USA
BVIW12n2257270316
441970BV00001B/1

* 9 7 8 0 9 9 7 1 0 5 9 1 9 *